T0298412

Commendations

If you ever wondered if Agile methodology can be applied to a sales environment, then this is the book for you. A step-by-step process explained from the point of view of someone who has walked the walk, not just talked the talk. A compelling read for anyone who wants to elevate their sales approach above the crowd.

Ken Aitken
Managing Director, SmartFreight

The sales function, once believed to be exempt from the requirement to practice continuous improvement, is struggling. Now shaken by the age of e-commerce, sales teams are looking for answers. *Agile Sales* provides a path forward.

Robert Hafey
Author, Lean Safety and Lean Safety Gemba Walks

What a great little book! For the first time, continuous improvement and sales have been effectively brought together in a practical and easily readable way. It covers all the key topics in improving sales: clear team direction, exceptional culture, systematic approach, helping customers to improve, leader standard work, coaching and support of your sales team, as well as mapping customers' personas and creating an empathy map. A must buy.

Prof. Peter Hines
Founder, SA Partners, and Shingo Publication Award-winning author
(Staying Lean and The Essence of Excellence)

An easy-to-read essential guide to the implementation of continuous improvement in the sales process with lots of practical tips and examples.

Chris Butterworth
Shingo Publication Award-winning author
(4+1 and The Essence of Excellence)

To my knowledge, there is no better practical guide for applying Agile in a sales environment. This book is filled with practical tips, useful techniques, and relatable stories for anyone who is working in a sales environment. Being in charge of a professional sales team with a very challenging sales target, I couldn't help but think I wished I had read it a year ago! The premise of Brad's work is simple. Sales is about understanding your customers intimately and findings ways to add value to them. Agile is also about understanding customers deeply and focusing everyone, in rapid iterations, to create customer value. This book is suitable for anyone who is interested in learning about Agile and applying it in a sales context.

Keivan Zokaei
Shingo Publication Award-winning author
(Creating a Lean and Green Business System)

Brad Jeavons's *Agile Sales*, which is part business development and part personal development, provides realistic knowledge and learning practices to understand the customer journey and realize the importance of the role that our values play toward appreciating this journey.

Shawn Kerr
General Manager, Battery World Australia Pty Ltd

Having witnessed first-hand Brad's passion for sales and Agile methodologies and shared his interest in making a positive change for almost a decade, I was looking forward to reading this book. If you are interested in how selling can deliver real value to your customers, which is repaid with loyalty and understanding, then this book is for you.

Neil Jorgensen
Marketing and Communications Manager, B&R Enclosures Pty Ltd

As our customers have access to more information and need to make purchasing decisions faster than ever, it becomes harder as a salesperson to keep up using traditional sales techniques. This book is a realistic and practical approach to deciding where to focus our sales efforts. By doing so, we can adapt and place our energy on where it should be. Brad has given the roadmap on how to succeed in an ever-changing market. This book is an essential read for any salesperson looking to stand out from the crowd.

Boyd Rose
Product Manager, insignia Pty Ltd

Brad has captured a range of practical business approaches incorporating sales techniques that change the paradigm as to how to better engage with customers in a valued way that can deliver sustainable results. I had the opportunity to see this approach in action during a visit to the Winson Group office after one of their sales teams engaged with our manufacturing business in such a unique way I was intrigued as to the business behind the approach. I was really impacted by the vibrancy and engagement of that team and the results they were generating. I would encourage salespersons in any business that has challenging markets, where lower price is the default position for sale teams, to read Brad's book and load their team on the *Agile Sales* bus that will lead to better business outcomes.

Lester Kirkwood
National Sales and Marketing Manager, Orrcon Steel

In the age of disruption, with a growing focus on customer-centricity, Brad provides a thorough roadmap, informing us what all sales leaders need to understand and execute to ensure their and their team's success. Born out of continuous improvement methodology, and with an overriding focus on cultural leadership, *Agile Sales* handles the complex and makes it straightforward, applicable, and executable.

Daniel Pirrone
Consultant, Six Degrees

If you're looking for practical tools to help you ignite your sales team, delight customers, and grow revenue, *Agile Sales* will give you of all that and more. I have had the pleasure of working with Brad for a number of years and have seen first-hand how these continuous improvement methodologies have helped teams to develop clarity of purpose, improve culture, and build highly effective sales teams with a focus on delivering customer value.

Karen Moon
General Manager, Market Strategy &
Communications, Madison Technologies

From graduates to seasoned salespersons, this book provides a concise, end-to-end recipe for sales success. I congratulate Brad on his book, and I commend this book to anyone who provides a product or a service for a customer.

Russell Warner
Strategic Partnership Manager, ETS Pty Ltd

Having been in businesses for many years, I've read plenty of business books. Had I read Brad's book first, I would not have needed to read many of the others. This book contains a goldmine of useful and practical advice, covering not only sales but also many other aspects. I particularly like the plethora of direct business examples, as well as the frequent summation of topics and useful actions all the way through the book.

David Cullen
Director, DC Automation

I have always found Brad to be engaging, empathetic, brilliant, questioning, passionate about his work, a great listener, and most importantly, natural and honest. When I was reading this book, Brad's passion flowed off the pages, and it felt like I was sitting down listening to him. The topics are extremely relevant today, and Brad has researched them well. They are presented concisely, finding a great balance between content, examples, and guides for implementation. Well done Brad, I am looking forward to your next book already!

Jason Goode
Packaging Manager, Reece Group

Brad Jeavons has crafted an excellent book that takes the concept of "sales" to its rightful place – a focus on the customer's journey and applying Agile principles in order to optimize an organization's pipeline of profitable sales delivering value to the customer. Brad shows his dual expertise in sales management and continuous improvement best practices and provides some great practical examples. Apply the disciplines and mindset described here, and be confident of sales flow: a sustainable and visible sales pipeline.

Jon Lindsay
Chair, The Executive Connection, and Principal, Joined-Up®

The world of sales has become increasingly challenging, customers demand more and the old ways are no longer good enough. Brad has created a toolkit that that brings together established methodologies with practical examples of how to apply them within a commercial environment. This book is an essential read for any sales leader.

Will Edwards
Director of Channels, Domino Printing Sciences

Agile Sales

Agile Sales
Delivering Customer Journeys of Value and Delight

Authored by
Brad Jeavons

Edited by
Emily Jeavons

A PRODUCTIVITY PRESS BOOK

First published 2020
by Routledge
52 Vanderbilt Avenue, New York, NY 10017

and by Routledge
2 Park Square, Milton Park, Abingdon, Oxon, OX14 4RN

Routledge is an imprint of the Taylor & Francis Group, an informa business

© 2020 Brad Jeavons

The right of Brad Jeavons to be identified as author of this work has been asserted by him in accordance with sections 77 and 78 of the Copyright, Designs and Patents Act 1988.

All rights reserved. No part of this book may be reprinted or reproduced or utilised in any form or by any electronic, mechanical, or other means, now known or hereafter invented, including photocopying and recording, or in any information storage or retrieval system, without permission in writing from the publishers.

Trademark notice: Product or corporate names may be trademarks or registered trademarks, and are used only for identification and explanation without intent to infringe.

Library of Congress Cataloging-in-Publication Data
Names: Jeavons, Brad, author.
Title: Agile sales : delivering customer journeys of value and delight /
Brad Jeavons.
Description: New York, NY : Routledge, 2020. | Includes bibliographical references and index.
Identifiers: LCCN 2019057246 (print) | LCCN 2019057247 (ebook) | ISBN 9780367417536 (paperback) | ISBN 9780367419424 (hardback) | ISBN 9780367816919 (ebook)
Subjects: LCSH: Selling. | Sales management. | Customer relations.
Classification: LCC HF5438.25 .J43 2020 (print) | LCC HF5438.25 (ebook) | DDC 658.85--dc23
LC record available at https://lccn.loc.gov/2019057246
LC ebook record available at https://lccn.loc.gov/2019057247

ISBN: 978-0-367-41942-4 (hbk)
ISBN: 978-0-367-41753-6 (pbk)
ISBN: 978-0-367-81691-9 (ebk)

Typeset in Garamond
by codeMantra

For my mother, Lorraine Beverley Jeavons (1949–2018),
who taught me so much.

Contents

List of Figures

Foreword

You might well ask why this book has a foreword from someone based in (Old) South Wales working in a higher education institute in Ireland. Well, the answer, to misquote slightly, is that it boldly goes where no book has gone before. I have been working in the improvement arena now for over 30 years and, like Brad, was heavily influenced by TQM (total quality management) and JIT (just-in-time) before spending many years running the Lean Enterprise Research Centre (LERC) at Cardiff University. At LERC, we had a number of aims, always taking a contingent approach to the topic. One such aim was to research how improvement could be applied right across the whole organization. Over the years, I have found many great examples in different functions, but until I met Brad, I had never seen a compelling example in sales.

Brad is a rare example in that he led the (then Lean) improvement activity in Winson from a background in sales. I took inspiration from what he did both within sales and the wider business. Within sales, I was impressed with how he trained and developed the team as well as how they applied visual management. However, I was equally inspired by how he led the improvement activity across the whole business.

In my own journey, I now tend to refer to improvement as "enterprise excellence" following the lead from the Shingo Institute and Association for Manufacturing Excellence (AME). This general term allows for local customization so that terms like Agile may be applied within office-based functions such as IT and sales where this language works well for those involved.

This book does two main things. Firstly, it effectively focuses the reader's attention onto all of the main core Management Systems required for a successful and sustainable transformation. These include:

1. Behavioral and Strategy Deployment
   a. Understanding the customer in terms of both persona and empathy
   b. Defining the behaviors required to be successful
   c. Deploying strategy through the executive, divisional, department, and individual levels
2. Continuous Improvement
   a. Using scrums to focus on the most appropriate short- and long-term improvement activities
   b. Applying PDCA (Plan, Do, Check, Act continuous improvement cycle)-based sprints and their prioritization
   c. Devising a pull-based pipeline using Kanban
3. Leader Standard Work
   a. Changing habits
   b. Focus leaders' time on the most important activities
   c. Sustaining focus
4. Learning and Development
   a. Developing the skills required for leader standard work
   b. Developing and coaching the team
   c. Helping people learn through storytelling

I would suggest you read through the first half of the book carefully and develop your plan of how you can apply this thinking, as the second half is dependent on you doing this. You may need to read it more than once, and I would also suggest you ask colleagues in other functions to read this as well and think about how they might apply the approach in their areas. Be careful that you don't leave the rest of the business behind!

Secondly, the book applies this thinking into the sales pipeline consisting of the key phases of "Discovery," "Research," "Purchase," "Delivery," and "Devotion." There are numerous examples as well as great tips. Personally, what I found useful was collecting the various insights Brad provides. Perhaps you might do the same and create your own framework of sales principles. Here is what I found:

1. Become a partner rather than a vendor.
2. Create multiple touch points.
3. Ask the right questions in the right way.
4. Elevate your conversations.
5. Listen empathetically.
6. Do a deep dive on key topics.

  7. Simplify the purchase.
  8. Motivate the purchase.
  9. Quote nashis not apples.
 10. Close with abundance.
 11. Collaborate to achieve excellence.
 12. Deliver, and continue to deliver, value and delight.

You might like to use your own list to guide you in reviewing how well you are doing at present and what you will seek to do in future.

   This is an excellent book. Brad has done a great job … oh, and he also likes nashis!

Professor Peter Hines
Waterford Institute of Technology, Ireland
Co-Author of The Essence of Excellence

Preface

I was introduced to sales at a young age listening as my mother, Lorraine, made weekly phone calls to her customers, gaining orders for our wholesale garden plant farm. She built strong personal relationships with her customers and knew their business, personal backgrounds, challenges, and future goals. Mum was an expert on plants and would help her customers to time their purchase as ideally as possible, especially with flowering varieties. She was focused on helping her customers achieve excellent outcomes.

Mum diarized her conversations with customers, their latest successes, challenges, and future goals. She would reference her diary before the next call and always bring into conversation what she had learned previously. The relationships she formed lasted well after the end of her time working in the industry. Watching her in action, I never saw sales in a bad light. I saw it as a process of helping customers achieve their goals through sales expertise.

I chose to study International Business at university, thinking at the time that I would focus on marketing and sales. I quickly diverted my focus to learning about operational excellence practices in Japan, known as Total Quality Management (TQM) and Toyota Production System (TPS). I became fascinated with the tools and techniques used to achieve higher quality, productivity, reduced lead times, and flexibility in operations, all with an absolute focus on the customer. I studied a concept called McDonaldization (Ritzer, 2008), which was focused on the techniques used by McDonald's to systemize in-store operations. McDonaldization enabled young people to deliver consistent quality and value to customers in a simple way. I was dreaming of leading a significant manufacturing facility, transforming it into the most efficient high-quality production facility ever to exist! Big dreams, I know!

Upon leaving university, I found myself in a graduate position with a growing Australian manufacturing and distribution company ... in a sales position! I took to it straight away and was trained in many techniques to sell our products better than the competition.

I was working with an experienced sales leader, John Brennan, who positively influenced my professional development. John exuded knowledge and experience in sales like a master craftsman. I learned from John the importance of focusing on the lead measures and doing the basics well to get results. I learned the importance of focus, that selling is a numbers game, and that the numbers you are chasing need to be focused on where you can get the best results. John coached me on critical sales skills and practices. He taught me to always stand in reception and to be prepared to greet your contact positively and professionally. He taught me how to effectively present my organization using quality visual sales tools.

John developed his sales leadership skills through a diverse career starting as a roustabout and, later, as a wool grader in the shearing sheds of western New South Wales in Australia. The environment of the shearing sheds was harsh and so were the people who worked in it. The work was hard, and you had to learn how to adapt and get on with the tough people around you to survive.

John eventually left the outback and returned to Sydney, where he entered the advertising market and started to learn the art of marketing and sales working for *Readers Digest*. *Readers Digest* in this era was the magazine of choice in Australia. It was an organization that had mastered the art of marketing, sales, and distribution. There was no better marketing and sales outfit than *Readers Digest*, allowing John to learn from the best.

Following this, John moved into the logistics industry in sales, learning skills at engaging with industrial and supply chain industries, operations, and warehouse managers selling logistics services. This was a different sales environment with new decision-makers having personas different to those of people engaged by *Readers Digest*. John adapted to this new industry quickly, achieved great success, and quickly became the State Manager.

John was then enticed by his brother, Mark, to join a family-owned Brisbane-based company, Ace Marking (which is now known as Signet). This is where I met John. Signet was, and still is, an innovative organization when it comes to sales and marketing, thanks in part to John.

It was a fantastic opportunity to work and learn from experienced senior marketing and sales professionals. There is so much to gain from these experts even in our era of rapidly changing technology. Sales are achieved by dealing with people now as it was hundreds of years ago. The people John dealt with in the early years of his career had similar baseline desires, needs, and goals as the people I have dealt with throughout my career. I thank John for all I learned from him, the hard work while we were clocked on, and good times we had after hours.

Early on in my career, I was leading a young team of graduates selling into the Auto-ID and data capture market. I knew more about the humble barcode than I ever thought I would. I put into practice what I had learned from John and the training we had been given.

The team had a vision – we wanted to become the largest in the market within five years. The team had a mission – Who Dares Wins – which we stole from the Special Air Services (SAS), a British army speciality forces unit. This was a bit corny for a sales team, but it fired us up. The team knew its point of difference, which revolved around reliability, ease of use, and servicing of the products we were selling as well as our sales process.

We steadily improved our leading measures and used our time productively. We achieved team sales conversion rates over 90%. We doubled our net sales annually and executed our vision within five years, which was an incredible achievement for such a young team with no prior sales experience.

Upon reflection, I believe the success that we had was attributable to having:

- clear team direction,
- an exceptional culture, and
- a systematic approach.

Our sales approach was highly product-focused, which I believe hindered us when we entered a new market through an acquisition. The company bought the distribution rights for an automated printing equipment manufacturer, Domino. This change brought us into the manufacturing industry, selling automated coding and labeling equipment used in factories for the identification and traceability of products as part of their quality control systems. We entered this market with a high level of confidence based on our past success and were smashed by one of the leading industry players.

Initially, we did not understand how this could be happening. We were doing everything we had previously done but kept getting beaten. Our conversion rate was only 40%, and we were only growing at 15% p.a.

Over time, we realized that this competitor was doing more than selling products (which was our focus). They were offering to truly help their customers improve in the areas their customers were most focused on.

Our competitor was selling at a strategic level to senior decision-makers. We could not access these high-level decision-makers because of our product sales focus, which top-level decision-makers were not interested in. This was a real learning curve for our team, and we took some time to correct ourselves due to our long-term focus on product sales.

At around this time, I was promoted to General Manager (GM), leading and improving an operational team. I had overlooked my university learnings in operational excellence from the time of my sales career and had a lot of catching up to do. The job promotion reignited my passion for learning. I studied everything that I could get my hands on relating to the topic of operational excellence. I discovered that the concept of TQM had been superseded by a concept called Lean. The ideas were similar, as both were built around best-practice operational excellence techniques. I rediscovered the heart of operational excellence – focusing on understanding what your customers value and, as a team, continuously improving toward this.

At first, I focused heavily on the operational side of the business, training and developing team members to understand who their internal and external customers were, what they valued, and how to continuously improve toward this. One day, it dawned on me that this is no different from what is needed to achieve excellence in sales. I had an aha moment when I realized that, ultimately, sales teams that perform at the highest level are improvement consultants helping customers improve toward their goals.

Sales teams go wrong when they purely focus on finding customer pain and then sell their products and services for them to overcome this pain. In this mode, we neglect the elevated focus areas of senior decision-makers. We don't gain an understanding of what these decision-makers are focused on strategically. Importantly, I looked at our sales team as being Continuous Improvement specialists in our areas of expertise for our customers.

We shifted our focus as a sales team from product sales to helping our customers improve in our areas of expertise. We were all trained in Lean and Theory of Constraints, two best-practice continuous improvement areas of theory, tools, and techniques. The younger team members embraced this new approach quickly and achieved amazing things.

Katie Shailes, one of our youngest team members, welcomed the new sales approach. Katie had limited product knowledge but did not let this hold her back. She worked hard to learn all there was to know about continuous improvement and the new sales process we had developed. She regularly sought out experienced team members and gained insights into these techniques from everyone she could. This ultimately led to a result that we never would have believed if we hadn't lived through it. Katie, through these efforts, produced the most significant first-year sales ever within a male-dominated, highly technical market. Well done, Katie!

The older sales team members who had been focused on product sales for so long found the transition more difficult. They were used to focusing on and pitching the products they were passionate about as part of their sales process. The issue we found was that the moment a salesperson launches into a product pitch, the opportunity to engage customers in a consultative way that builds value and trust is destroyed.

Further training backed by longer-term ride-along coaching and support was the technique we used to help team members transition. We focused on assisting them in evolving from their traditional product-focused approach. Our goal was to help them form new sales habits in a consultative sales approach to help customers achieve their goals. Some salespeople could not make the transition and chose to leave. Others, though, embraced the new consultative approach and worked hard to learn new skills and overcome their old product sales habits.

My career changed again. After a few years in the GM role, I transitioned into a Business Improvement Manager for the broader group I worked for. I still hadn't lost my passion for learning. I sought out broadening my knowledge in a new area of excellence I had just discovered: Agile. Agile is a continuous improvement/project management approach that had been embraced by many of the world's largest and most successful organizations.

The real learning came for me through courses run by marketing professionals who were developing Agile in new directions to deliver customer value as well as delight. Agile focuses on improvement in the conscious value areas for customers (which Lean had previously driven), as well as on their emotional drivers. This dual approach of value and delight and continuous improvement to enhance customer experience takes business improvement and performance to a whole new level.

My journey has brought me to this place – applying Agile to sales to help sales teams and organizations deliver customer journeys of value and delight.

This book will provide sales leaders and teams with the knowledge and techniques I have gained through my journey to this point. I hope that you, as a reader, learn many ideas to take back and help your team and organization improve for your customers.

Acknowledgments

First, I must acknowledge my wife, Emily. Without her advice, immense efforts, and editing prowess, this book would never have eventuated. In addition, I must recognize Russell Warner, who helped me focus and achieve clarity of thought for this book. Over several years and many campfire drinks, Russell challenged and helped me format essential concepts for this book.

Acknowledgments must also go to the inspirational people I have worked with over the years. Thanks to Jack Winson, John Brennan, John King, Boyd Rose, James Poulsen, Suzie Young, Andy Hecke, and Michael Shaw, who have played such a significant role in my career. Many thanks to Dan Pirrone, who has helped me immensely throughout this book-writing journey and with the contribution on running value-add events.

Thanks to the contributors on operational excellence throughout my career, with a special note to Peter Hines, Chris Butterworth, Alex Teoh, Bob Simpson, and Bob Hafey. I appreciate the knowledge and support you have provided me over the years.

I finally want to acknowledge all the customers and colleagues I have worked with, learnt from, and achieved great things with over the years. Teamwork and collaboration will always achieve more than the individual, and I have been extremely fortunate to experience amazing outcomes in this area throughout my career.

About the Author

Brad Jeavons is an Organization Improvement Leader whose purpose is *helping people reach their potential*. He is focused on assisting organizations achieve excellence for their people, customers, society, and the planet.

Over the past 20 years, Brad has accumulated extensive experience in leadership, sales, manufacturing, logistics, and consulting. He has worked with leading organizations across a broad range of industries such as retail, transport, technology, automotive, food and beverage, health, finance, and many more.

Brad's passion for helping people led him to become a writer. Brad's wide range of expertise has combined to provide unique insights and knowledge toward achieving organizational excellence. His first book, *Agile Sales*, has been developed from his experience in operational and sales excellence. Brad, for many years, had seen salespeople becoming disrupted by technology such as online stores and knowledge sharing systems. His book *Agile Sales* provides salespeople and organizations approaches to build agility and start delivering value to customers again.

Brad believes that successful organizational transformation requires more than just improvement to processes. It also requires a strong focus on leadership, behavior, and culture to sustain.

Brad welcomes your contact and thoughts via his website: www.iqi.com.au

Introduction

Today's Sales Challenge

Salespeople are becoming disrupted in the same way that taxi drivers have been by Uber and hotel staff by Air BnB. We are all customers in this world of information technology. Many of us know how easy it is to extensively research our needs before we even engage a salesperson. Product- and price-focused salespeople have limited value to offer to a customer who has done extensive online research on products available to meet their needs.

This is a demotivating place to be in as a salesperson. The result is a transient salesforce continually moving from one job to another. Salespeople search for a market where they can continue to sell purely based on relationships, product, and price. This does not result in a positive change at all. Salespeople need to find a new way to deliver value to customers other than product and pricing knowledge.

Leading organizations and their salespeople have made the changes needed. They have embraced Agile philosophy and techniques and have shifted into a position of offering value and delight to their customers.

What Is Agile?

The Agile approach was initially developed at the Harvard Business School in 1986 by Hirotaka Takeuchi and Ikujiro Nonaka. They published an article in the *Harvard Business Review* called "The New Product Development Game" (Nonaka and Takeuchi, 1986). Takeuchi and Nonaka studied manufacturers who were releasing new innovations far quicker than traditionally possible. They studied organizations achieving this, such as Fuji-Xerox, Honda, and Canon. What they found and detailed was a rugby-style approach to innovation that incorporated a cross-functional team structure with teams working as one. They observed these teams passing information and support back and forth to each other (similar to ball passing in a game of rugby). This was totally different from the traditional relay race approach to product development where one team does their part and then passes the baton onto the next team to perform their role in the product development process.

This cross-functional team approach had a specific feature – regular, rapid, and often stand-up meetings rather than the traditional weekly or fortnightly long project meeting. These short, sharp project meetings enabled teams to identify and overcome challenges quickly before they became big problems. It also gave the teams a higher level of focus on and constant energy for the project. The results demonstrated a fast, flexible, innovating organization which led to the use of the term "Agile."

Many of our largest, most well-known information technology brands have achieved great things through teams utilizing Agile. These organizations have implemented Agile techniques to build a culture of continuous innovation. Agile is now being adopted within leading sales teams to differentiate themselves and to avoid commoditization and replacement by online stores and websites.

Agile has grown holistically over time, enabling teams and organizations to achieve excellence.

In today's market, there are seven general concepts of an Agile Sales organization (Figure I.1):

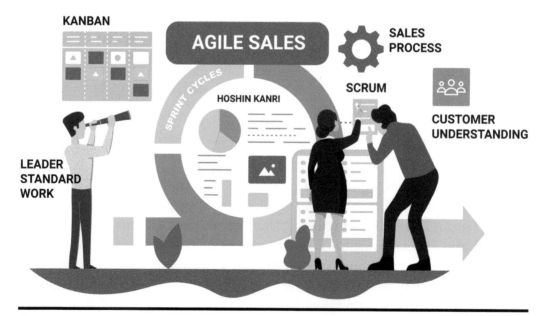

Figure I.1   Agile Sales.

1. **Customer Understanding** – providing value and delight.
2. **Hoshin Kanri** – aligning and engaging everyone in innovation.
3. **Scrum** – rapid visual performance meetings.
4. **Kanban** – visual improvement and sales project management.
5. **Sprints** – rapid iterative experimentation.
6. **Leader Standard Work** – Leading Excellence.
7. **Sales Process** – aligned to the customer's buying journey.

We will explore each of these concepts in this book, providing an understanding of an Agile Sales organization. We will explore each topic together with case examples, providing tips and tricks to help you and your team enhance the value and delight you offer your customers now and into the future.

Chapter 1

Agile Sales Concept 1: Customer Understanding

Many organizational excellence approaches such as Lean, Six Sigma, and Agile all concentrate on understanding what customers value. Agile goes one step further, as it also considers what brings customers delight. Agile recognizes that emotional experience is equally as important as the perceived value that the customer experiences when engaging with your brand. Emotional experience interacts with the limbic brain, which is directly involved in decision-making.

Agile focuses on knowing who your customers are and then putting yourself in their shoes to truly, empathically understand them. It becomes simple to learn how to deliver higher value and delight through this empathic understanding.

In this chapter, we will cover the following tools that you can use to analyze who your customers indeed are:

1. The Pareto Principle – understanding who your top customers are
2. The Persona Map – deeply understanding key decision-makers
3. Contextual Interview – gaining direct insights
4. Empathy Map – living in their shoes.

Utilizing these tools will offer you insights into how you can deliver a higher level of value and delight to your ideal customers.

The Pareto Principle

The Pareto Principle was developed by Vilfredo Pareto (Pareto, 1896) in 1896. Pareto was a sociologist and economist and developed the Pareto theory while studying land distribution in his home country, Italy. He found that most of the land in Italy was owned by a few, and this dropped rapidly down to a small amount of property owned by the masses.

Pareto developed the rapidly declining bar graph of the distribution shown in Figure 1.1.

The Pareto Principle has been found to accurately describe many situations, such as the significant contributors to quality defects and safety incidents in a workplace, to hospital emergency department cases at a particular time of the week, to sales and profit revenue from customers, to items produced and sold by an organization.

The Pareto Principle can help an organization understand where they have been and could be most successful with the least amount of resource. It highlights why an organization and its people get distracted with the (often large) tail of smaller customers rather than focusing upon where they can be most successful. This tail can bring a great deal of noise and distraction if not effectively managed.

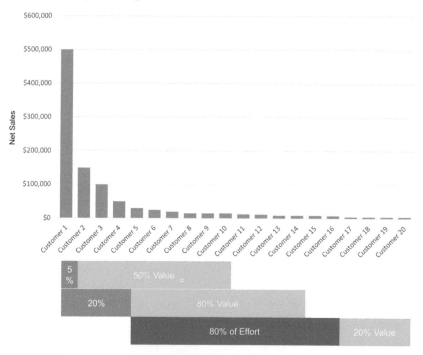

Figure 1.1   Pareto Principle and 80/20 Rule.

To conduct a Pareto analysis, simply generate a database of your sales by your customers over a recent period, say a few months or a year. Sort the database from largest to smallest, and then chart it using a bar graph, and hey presto, you have a Pareto analysis! With this data, it is crucial to analyze the top customers that you have had so much success with, and why you have had this success. The trick is to focus on your top 1%–5% of customers, which I predict will be bringing you between 30% and 50% of your sales. Get things right with these top-end customers first.

There are some great Agile tools and techniques that can help an organization gain a better understanding of customers. They can create an understanding of why customers purchase from your organization and what would keep them buying from you long into the future.

Living in Their Shoes

I have engaged with so many people throughout my career who talk about customers as if they are brands, buildings, or even mystical non-living entities! The reality is that customers are people like you and me. The problem of viewing customers as being objects rather than people creates a "one approach suits all" mentality of dealing with customers. We know that we are all different; we all want to be treated as individuals rather than one of the masses. When we are treated as an individual by someone tailoring to our needs, we experience delight and perceive high value from the interaction.

How does a business strategically plan and improve toward their customers? There are techniques for achieving this, and we will cover these throughout the rest of this book.

At a high level in Agile, we look to group people into typical personas that engage with our brand. When you analyze a group of people, you will find differences within everyone. You will also find a lot of commonalities that allow you to group and develop knowledge based on these groupings. In Agile, we call these groupings of related people who engage with our products and services "personas."

Tools for Understanding Your Customer More Deeply

The Persona Map

Typically, an organization will find that five to ten key customer personas engage with their brand and provide the most significant value (sales/profit)

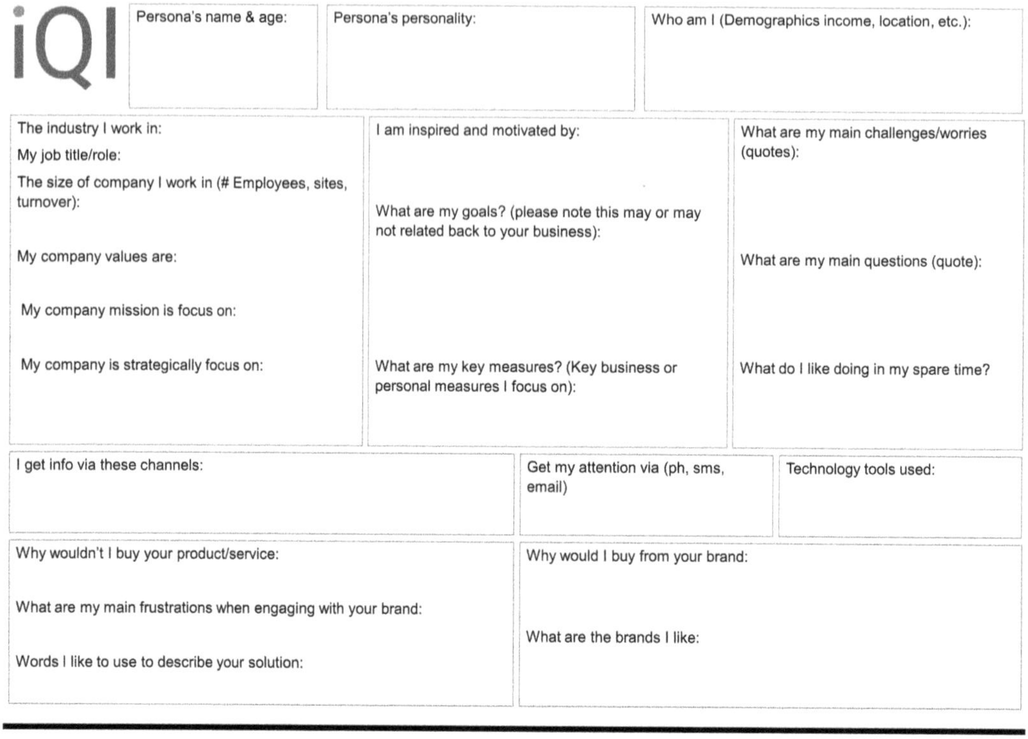

iQI

Persona's name & age:

Persona's personality:

Who am I (Demographics income, location, etc.):

The industry I work in:

My job title/role:

The size of company I work in (# Employees, sites, turnover):

My company values are:

My company mission is focus on:

My company is strategically focus on:

I am inspired and motivated by:

What are my goals? (please note this may or may not related back to your business):

What are my key measures? (Key business or personal measures I focus on):

What are my main challenges/worries (quotes):

What are my main questions (quote):

What do I like doing in my spare time?

I get info via these channels:

Get my attention via (ph, sms, email)

Technology tools used:

Why wouldn't I buy your product/service:

What are my main frustrations when engaging with your brand:

Words I like to use to describe your solution:

Why would I buy from your brand:

What are the brands I like:

Figure 1.2   Persona Map.

in return. The Agile tool that is used to help a team define their key personas is called a Persona Map.

In Figure 1.2, you will see some of the standard groupings of information that a team looks for to understand the different individuals they engage. Standard data captured includes age, demographics, personality, industry, company characteristics, motivations and goals, challenges and questions, communication channels and tools, as well as information about what they typically do and don't like about your brand.

You can download this Persona Map for your immediate use at www.iqi.com.au.

The way to capture this data is to take the top grouping of Pareto customers from your database. Analyze the key decision-makers through existing data and input from team members within your organization. You can use social media tools and general Google searches to start to build an understanding of these decision-makers and begin to identify common traits.

Example – Driven Bob Persona Map

An excellent example of the use of the Pareto analysis technique followed by a Persona Map was conducted by a long-time colleague of mine, Boyd Rose. Boyd was brave enough in the early days of my discovery of this approach to conduct these analyses with me to discover his ideal customers.

Boyd was selling industrial equipment into Australian manufacturers and warehouses. Boyd brought together several experienced teammates (who dealt directly with customers) to review the Pareto chart information for his customers. These colleagues helped define common characteristics and groupings for both the companies and decision-makers within them. The team focused on the top 5% of Boyd's customers, which equated for over 60% of his annual sales.

They drew on several resources to help them research and develop a profile:

■ Their knowledge and experience with the companies and decision-makers;
■ The company web sites for background information;
■ Google searches for articles and additional data;
■ Annual Reports for directional information such as purpose/mission, vision, and critical strategies and measures; and
■ LinkedIn, Facebook, and general Google searches for decision-maker persona information.

Throughout this process, Boyd and his team were able to find a clear grouping of two ideal customer organizations where he has had most success:

1. Food and beverage manufacturers with
   – Over $500 million turnover,
   – At least 10 production lines nationally (could be multi-site),
   – A culture focused on innovation and continuous improvement,
   – Strategic direction concentrated on quality and productivity gains, and
   – A focus on production line performance.
2. Building product manufacturers with
   – Over $200 million turnover,
   – At least three production lines nationally,
   – A culture focused on innovation and continuous improvement,
   – Strategic direction concentrated on quality and productivity improvement, and
   – A focus on production line performance.

Figure 1.3 Personal Map of Driven Bob.

When analyzing the decision-makers, the team found several key personas. Their most important of these was a persona they called Driven Bob (Figure 1.3).

The Persona Map details much information about Driven Bob, such as

- Job roles = Factory/Plant Leader/GM Operations,
- Mid-level introverted personality,
- Middle–upper income, living in the outer suburbs,
- Motivated by achieving goals and measures such as:
  - Productivity measures (such as overall equipment effectiveness (OEE)),
  - Quality (right first time),
  - Safety measures (such as total recordable injury frequency rate (TRIFR), lost time injury (LTI) and medically treated incident (MTI)),
  - Culture (employee engagement survey),

- Major concerns and focus area on safety and line performance, and
- Looking for partners to help him overcome challenges and achieve his teams' goals.

The team now had a clear understanding of where Boyd had been most successful in the past. They then looked at all of the customers who purchased in Boyd's territory and were able to find some companies in the tail of the list (not purchasing much from Boyd yet), who resembled his ideal customer. They were able to research to find the "Bobs" for these companies. (It is always best to start building a target list of ideal customers from the companies who already deal with you. You will find ideal customers further down your list spending less with you currently; their potential has just not yet been realized.)

From this work Boyd was able to develop a quality target list of ideal customers. He improved his sales process using the knowledge he had gained through the process of defining Bob and focused on his ideal customers. Boyd went on to exceed his budget by at least 20% every year following and is still going!

This case example shows the power of understanding who your ideal personas are and improving your approach in delivering them higher value and delight. This approach has two benefits:

1. It focuses a salesperson on where they can find the highest return for their effort.
2. It allows the salesperson to improve and tailor their approach to these personas to truly create a point of difference in the market and deliver these personas value and delight.

The Contextual Interview

The next step is to meet with these customers and conduct a Contextual Interview.

A Contextual Interview is a meeting with a customer, typically one on one. During this meeting, you can check the data within your Persona Map and ask other important questions about their experiences with your organization and even your competitors.

The Contextual Interview form (Figure 1.4; Hines and Butterworth, 2019) can be used to discover what your customers value most. The approach will also help you find out innovative ways to improve for your customers into the future.

What do you value most from a supplier	Priority	Why is this valued?	Our performance (1-3)	Our nearest competitor performance (1-3)
Value for money	3	We need to reduce costs to stay competitive in our market.	3	2
Quality product and supply performance	1	It could stop production which costs $10K/hour.	2	2
Rapid support when I need it	2	I need to keep the production line running ($10K/hour downtime cost).	1	3
Think of the best supplier you have ever worked with, why were they so good?		What are you key goals, strategies & measures for the future?	Why are you focusing on these goals and strategies?	
They ran improvement collaboratively with our business to help us year after year.		Improve cost competitiveness. Key measure cost/unit produced.	We are getting beaten on price by over seas suppliers	
They trained us to be able to service their equipment ourselves.		Improve quality. Key measure cost of quality.	Our quality is currently comparable to our competitors, we need it to be better.	

Figure 1.4 Customer Contextual Interview Form.

Using this system, you simply ask the persona you are meeting, "What do you value most from a supplier?" Capture three to five responses, and then ask them to rank these in order of priority. The first answer someone makes is not necessarily the most important for them. Asking "Why?" or "What is it that makes each response vital to you?" a few times will help you get to a deeper understanding, which can be extremely powerful. You can also ask the customer to rank your performance and that of your competitors.

Example – Contextual Interview

I experienced this directly when one of our customers ranked us the lowest for "rapid support when I need it." We were ranked one (the lowest), while our competitor was ranked three (the highest).

We supplied manufacturers with automation equipment to identify their products. This customer always told us that our speed of response to a breakdown was critical to them. We had been fighting it out for years against competitors who were promising unachievable technician response time. We also saw traffic in cities worsening and didn't want to guarantee our customers response times we could not consistently deliver upon.

Our team conducted a Contextual Interview with key maintenance personas within the customer's sites. When we probed into technical response times, we discovered the substantial costs our customers incurred when their production lines stopped due to equipment failure. The losses were significant, often more than $10,000.00/hour. It usually took two to three hours to get to a customer's site from the time they logged a call with us, and our equipment only cost $15,000/unit. This insight enabled us to develop a failover solution. This meant that if one piece of equipment failed, another would automatically kick into action, avoiding any production downtime. Considering the cost of production downtime, the return on investment (ROI) was excellent, and our customer experience skyrocketed.

The bottom section of the survey (Figure 1.4) is forward or future-looking, enabling you to be ahead of the game. The "best supplier" question can provide a unique vision of innovative improvements your industry has not yet discovered. The "future goals, strategies, and measures" provide insight into where your customers want to move into the future, allowing you to improve in line with this. Again, asking "Why?" or "What is the reason for this strategy?" will provide you a more in-depth understanding.

The Empathy Map

The Persona Map and Contextual Interview provide you with data and strategic insights and ideas. Using this information, an Empathy Map will give you a catalyst for cultural change.

The Empathy Map (Figure 1.5) encourages you to truly live in the customer's shoes and show empathy to their situation. You will think deeply about what a customer is thinking and feeling day to day, noting down any ideas and thoughts that come to mind. You will think about what they see and hear and about their attitude. You can then think about what their major pains are and what would bring them the most significant gains.

This is a powerful approach, enabling team members to live in their customer's shoes and honestly think from the customer's perspective. I have not yet found a team that has not gained surprising insights from this exercise.

You can download this Empathy Map for your immediate use at www.iqi.com.au.

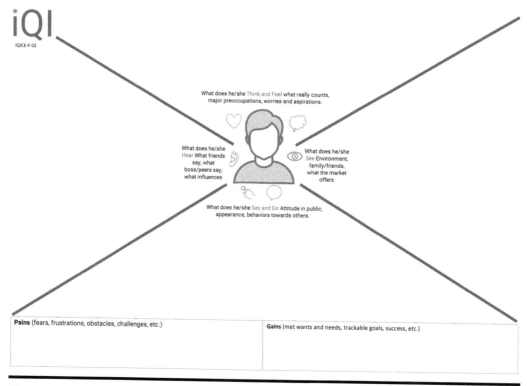

Figure 1.5   Empathy Map.

Service Safari

A Service Safari is a fantastic exercise that can be even more powerful than the Empathy Map. It requires a team member to become their customer: to go and work in their customer's site/s for a while, logging onto their own website at the customer's site, and attempting to look up items and place orders.

Shadowing

Shadowing is another equally powerful approach. Shadowing involves going to where your customers work or interact with your brand and simply observing what they are doing, thinking, and hypothesizing about what they may be feeling.

Example – Shadowing

One great example I saw was a significant transportation company within QLD who sent their team out into the field to shadow customers at train and bus stations. The first step they took was to find a prominent location to base themselves that provided a clear view of the station. They then noted down any significant observations they made relating to customer experiences, either good or bad. What they learned shocked them. They saw customers looking lost, searching for information to guide them where they needed to go. They saw customers having challenges with ticketing machines with queues of unhappy customers growing behind them. Most concerning was seeing elderly customers struggling to get onto transportation due to a large step from the station to the bus. The learnings from this initiative resulted in improvements that revolutionized the way the organization deployed information signage, used ticketing systems and improved customer transport boarding.

These approaches take a bit of time, but the insights they provide, and the cultural change that they promote is fantastic. I always encourage the taking of copious notes or voice recorded observations of any of your thoughts, discoveries, and opportunities for improvement during these events. Team members typically come back with a treasure trove of opportunities to deliver higher value and delight for their customers. There is no more robust approach to culture change and strategic improvement than living in your customer's shoes and genuinely showing empathy.

There are other great tools and techniques available within the Agile tool kit to help a team live in their customer's shoes, foster culture change, and innovate. The approaches I have covered are some of the critical tools and techniques, but please feel free to join our blog at iqi.com.au to discover more.

You can also download many of the forms that I have discussed in this section of the book at *www.iqi.com.au.*

Suggested Actions for Customer Understanding

1. Conduct a Pareto analysis of your customers or target customers. Define the top 5% of customers and the key decision-makers within these.
2. As a team, group these decision-makers based on shared traits.
3. Develop a Persona Map for the key three to five groupings identified.
4. Conduct one or more of the following activities to develop further understanding:
   - Contextual interview
   - Empathy map
   - Service safari
   - Shadowing

Chapter 2

Agile Sales Concept 2: Hoshin Kanri

The second concept of Agile is Hoshin Kanri. Hoshin Kanri is a strategic and financial planning, deployment, and execution process that originated in Japan. The process is linked to teachings provided in Japan throughout the 1950s by American Professors Edwards Deming and Peter Drucker. Deming and Drucker were brought into Japan by industry leaders to help support the redevelopment and growth of Japan after World War II (WWII), and they did a great job.

Hoshin Kanri enables the engagement and alignment of employees at all levels of the organization toward a clear strategic and financial direction and plan.

The process looks a lot like a waterfall of plans cascading through the organization while sustaining alignment to the top line plan. This is achieved by passing plans up and down the organization for review and adjustment before they are agreed upon and circulated. A great author on this topic, Pascal Dennis, coined the term "Catch Ball" (Dennis, 2006) for this process. Dennis noted that the process is a lot like passing a ball up and down the organization (Figure 2.1). The first ball that is passed is the top line executive plan. Once this is established, middle management plans are formed in alignment with the top line plan and again passed up, down and potentially across the organization for review and feedback. This process continues right down to individual plans of front-line employees. This process creates engagement, understanding, and through this, builds the foundation for ownership and accountability in delivering the plans.

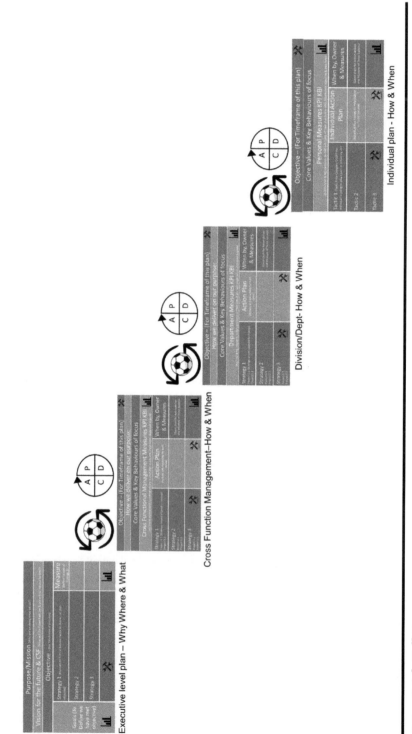

Figure 2.1 Catch Ball Process.

Executive Level Plan

To begin, a top-line plan is developed by the executive team that captures the mission/purpose, vision, and objectives for the organization. The plan outlines critical strategies to sustain or develop unique points of difference for their customers. The plan outlines critical success factors (measures) that they believe will help them achieve their strategies and objective. Measures drive behavior, and even top-level executives need clear measures of improvement to help guide their efforts and inform them that their efforts are working. The draft plan will then be passed to the other levels of the organization for review and feedback.

Feedback will be reviewed by the executive and relevant adjustments made. This process can occur many times in finalizing the top-line plan. You might be thinking to yourself, "I don't have time for that." The reason you put time into this process is to save time and frustration down the track. The Catch Ball process instantly starts to build an understanding of the plan at lower levels. The process always provides senior leaders with new insights from the lower levels that they had no idea about, which enhances the plan. The reason for taking the extra time early on in the planning process is to create empowerment within the organization. The approach of asking team members for their feedback and actively using this information creates an aligned, empowered organization. I believe that accountability can't be achieved without empowerment. Empowering and involving team members early on in the planning process creates a motivated, engaged team that is willing to be held to account.

Humility is the fundamental characteristic that enables a successful Catch Ball approach. This is a simple yet not easy approach to take. It requires all leaders of the organization to ask their employees, "What do you think about the plan we have put together so far?" and then discussing with them why there is a focus on these areas. Leaders need to respond to employees' responses by thanking them for the feedback and letting them know that it will be valued and reviewed. The plan then needs to be adjusted and shared with the team.

Hoshin Kanri also requires team members to show respect to their leaders when they start forming their plans aligned to the finalized top-level plan. Team members show respect by stating, "This is the plan we have formed based on your plan and our reasons why. What are your thoughts?" It takes a culture of respecting every individual's views and capabilities to succeed.

Divisional Team Plans

Once the top-level plan is finalized, executive leaders then support divisional teams to develop their aligned plans to help achieve the top-line business plan. Critical aspects of these divisional plans include strategically aligned projects and measures (lead and lag). These measures must be linked to the executive critical success factors to create alignment and ultimately help achieve the top-line plan. These plans will again be passed up, down, and also across (cross-functionally) the organization for review and feedback. Adjustments will be made to the plans as a result of this feedback. The organization now has a top-line executive plan and aligned divisional plans which are becoming more detailed concerning projects and measures. The next level of department plans will become even more tactical and detailed.

Department (Front-Line) Plans

The same process applies to department or front-line team plans. Divisional leaders assist department/front-line leaders and teams in developing their own aligned plans. Front-line plans are more tactical, focused on identifying critical measures for continuous improvement enabling the organization to achieve its objectives, move toward its vision, and live its mission and culture. These plans will be passed up and across the organization for review and feedback, after which adjustments will be made.

Individual Plans

Individual plans that are aligned to the department plan are then formed. Employees will define the projects that they are keen to help with and measures they believe they can focus upon to help achieve their departmental plans. The individual plan is again passed up and across the organization for review, feedback, and adjustment. Reaching this level of planning where an individual has an aligned annual plan is extremely powerful. More people exist at the front line of an organization than senior leadership. Hoshin Kanri that effectively cascades down to the individual employee focuses and engages every mind, body, and heart within the organization. This will always outperform strategic planning that sits with only a few people at the top of an organization.

Lead and Lag Measures

Lead measures are essential in achieving strategic performance and play a large part in the success or failure of strategy execution. Measures of performance come in two forms: lead and lag. Lag measures are the resulting measures we are seeking to achieve, such as sales results, gross profit, and net profit. They are called lag measures because, by the time we see the results, it is too late to improve; the result has already eventuated. Lead measures are based on the actions and behaviors we are planning to perform to deliver the results.

An example of a lag measure we may all experience is the desire to measure and lose weight. Weight loss is the lag measure. It will only be achieved through leading activities and behaviors, such as exercise (distance walked each day) and diet (kilojoules consumed). An individual measuring and working to improve their amount of exercise, and diet, will have a higher chance of performance in weight loss than an individual purely focused on the lag measure of weight loss. There is more chance the individual merely measuring weight loss will not do and improve upon the right leading measures to achieve the result. There is also a higher chance they get disgruntled and despondent when weight loss decline slows, which has been shown to occur over time.

The same concepts apply to business, especially in sales. If we only focus on the results (lag measures), we will have high likelihood of negative impacts such as demotivation and fluctuations in performance.

If, on the other hand, we focus on improving lead measures, we will give ourselves a much better chance of successfully and consistently delivering exceptional results. Examples of lead measures include the number of new customer connections, customer visits, dollars in opportunities raised, and opportunity pipeline movement/progression.

If, as a team, you have been improving a lead measure for some time with no result to the lag measure, don't stress. Simply predict other lead measures you could focus on to drive the result and change your focus. Lead measures encourage teams to plan ahead and work strategically. They empower teams to flex and change as required to execute strategy, sustain points of difference, and compete.

Strategy execution requires us, at all organizational levels, to create a forum for team members to communicate on strategic measures and projects to deliver the overall plan. Teams who do not meet to converse about strategic projects and measures will achieve very little, and plans will become dust collectors.

This forum for connection, named a Scrum, is detailed in the next chapter.

Suggested Actions for Hoshin Kanri

1. Take your vision, purpose/mission, strategic plan, and critical success factors (measures) and have a conversation with your team explaining why these focus areas have been chosen. Ask for your team's feedback on the plan. Make appropriate adjustments to your plan again, providing feedback.
2. Ask your team how they can help to achieve the company's vision, while keeping the mission in mind.
3. Discuss the critical few improvement projects (use 80/20 rule concept) the team could work upon to help achieve the strategic plan.
4. Define the critical lead and lag measures that the team could strategically improve upon to help achieve the critical success factors and meet the company's objectives.
5. Form a simple plan detailing the projects and measures the team want to focus on. Take this document to your leadership for review and feedback.
6. Continue the cascade to your front-line team and then the individual using the Catch Ball approach.

Chapter 3

Agile Sales Concept 3: Scrum

History of the Scrum

The concept of Scrum was first detailed by Takeuchi and Nonaka (Nonaka and Takeuchi, 1986) in their *Harvard Business Review* (HBR) journal article in 1986 that I have previously mentioned. They observed product development teams regularly huddling together for rapid visual meetings (RVMs), which they viewed as being similar to a Rugby Scrum, hence the name. The approach to Scrum that revolutionized product development and innovation within software companies was developed by Jeff Sutherland and Ken Schwaber in the mid-1990s. It has been documented within their Scrum guide (Schwaber and Sutherland, 2016). You can find great resources and information relating to Scrum from Jeff's company Scrum Inc. (Scruminc.com).

In many organizations, the Scrum for rapid new product design has merged with the Huddle (lean meeting approach) of RVMs. This allows for the development of culture, daily challenges to be solved, and continuous focus on improving execution of strategy.

In Sales

Sales teams have become part of this evolution, adopting the RVM concept to help build team culture and performance. By using RVMs, sales teams have been able to develop predictability and agility and analyze both lead and lag measures. By consistently focusing on lead measures, sales teams can predict critical indicators that determine the success or possible failure ahead of time. Team members can support each other in continuous improvement to help each other, and the team as a whole grows and succeeds.

Throughout the Entire Organization

All levels of an organization use the RVM approach to provide for issue and idea escalation and handling which genuinely creates an Agile organization.

RVM meetings run for 10–15 minutes. Information flows up and down the organization using the area leaders. For example, the leader of the front-line team takes any issues or improvement ideas they can't resolve to the next level RVM (Figure 3.1).

In an organization not running this approach, issues and strategic projects disappear, get lost in the noise, and typically chaos rules. The multi-level RVM approach enables improvement ideas and concerns to rapidly reach the level required to be dealt with promptly. The speed of information flow and support from all levels of the organization play a large part in creating a focused, Agile culture.

In companies that run a daily RVM approach, front-line teams will meet at the start of the day. There are typically many front-line teams in

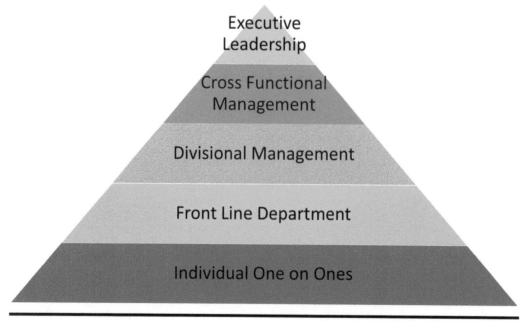

Figure 3.1   Multi-Level RVMs.

a large organization. The number of teams and and the number of RVMs reduce as you rise higher up the organization. With as little as a 5 minute gap, front-line team leaders will attend the divisional management team RVM. The divisional managers will then join the management or cross-functional management RVM, and finally, an executive RVM will occur.

With this structure, information can flow from the front-line huddle to the executive level within 1 hour (10 minute RVM, 5 minute gap between RVMs). This structure creates a truly Agile organization, as improvement ideas or issues can rapidly reach the area they need to, to be actioned. These ideas and concerns are captured visually and managed with actions or projects to ensure they are achieved. Sometimes a senior team will receive an issue or improvement idea from a lower-level team that can't be actioned immediately. When this occurs, the reason *why* must be communicated promptly to the originating team. This message is cascaded through the leadership channels like the idea and issue escalation approach.

How to Establish an RVM

Visual data is key to running a productive RVM. This visual data can be displayed on a manual or electronic board, depending on what is most appropriate.

Visual boards can display

- Cultural data and measures,
- Strategic projects and measures,
- Day-to-day operational measures,
- An action/project list for issues and improvement ideas which can be achieved within a few days, and
- A Kanban board (explained in the next chapter) to effectively manage longer-term improvements.

A schematic of this structure is shown in Figure 3.2.

An RVM visual board uses a traffic light system of red and green within the status columns and on the trend-line charts, clearly showing where you are winning or losing. The traffic light approach plays a significant role in creating a rapidly focused meeting. If a measure is green, it does not need to be discussed unless a team member deserves recognition or has knowledge to share about an extraordinary outcome or improvement. A red measure

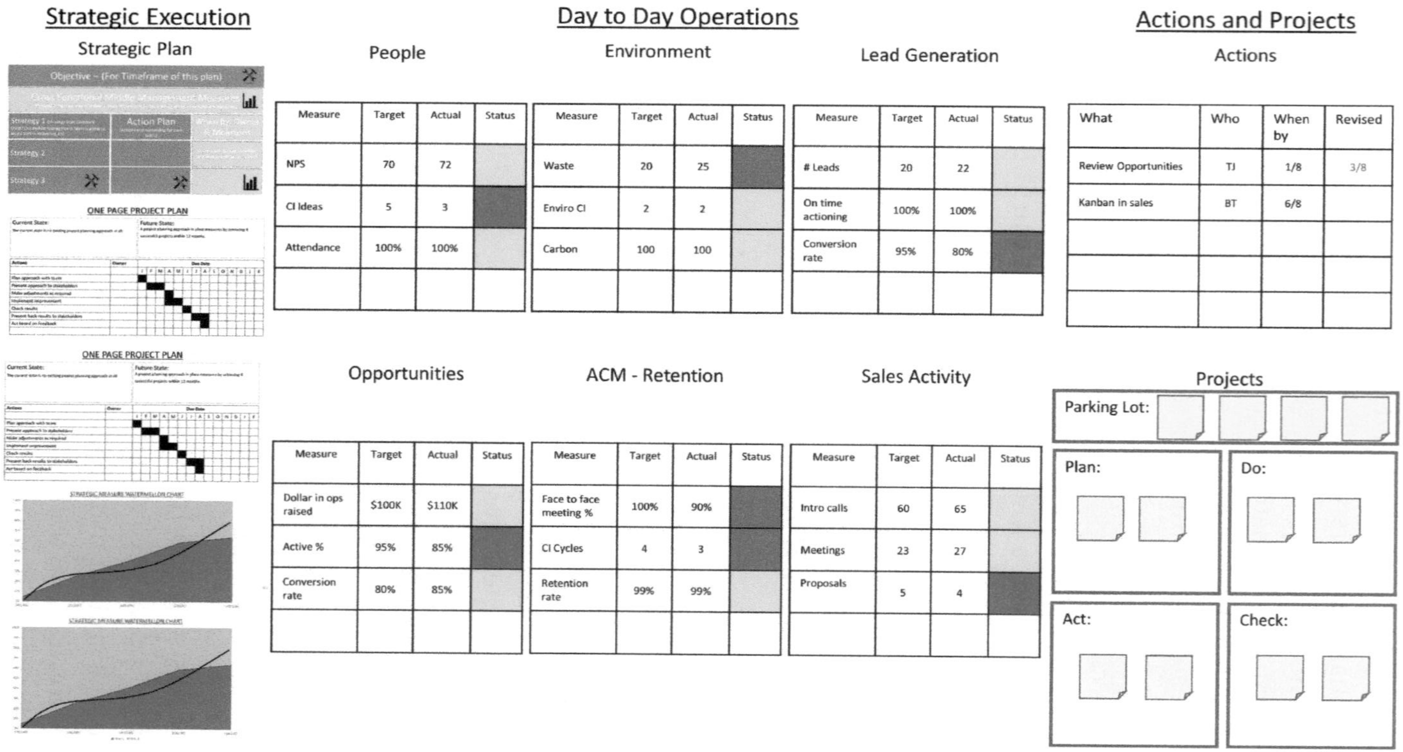

Strategic Execution

Strategic Plan

Day to Day Operations

People

Measure	Target	Actual	Status
NPS	70	72	
CI Ideas	5	3	
Attendance	100%	100%	

Environment

Measure	Target	Actual	Status
Waste	20	25	
Enviro CI	2	2	
Carbon	100	100	

Lead Generation

Measure	Target	Actual	Status
# Leads	20	22	
On time actioning	100%	100%	
Conversion rate	95%	80%	

Opportunities

Measure	Target	Actual	Status
Dollar in ops raised	$100K	$110K	
Active %	95%	85%	
Conversion rate	80%	85%	

ACM - Retention

Measure	Target	Actual	Status
Face to face meeting %	100%	90%	
CI Cycles	4	3	
Retention rate	99%	99%	

Sales Activity

Measure	Target	Actual	Status
Intro calls	60	65	
Meetings	23	27	
Proposals	5	4	

Actions and Projects

Actions

What	Who	When by	Revised
Review Opportunities	TJ	1/8	3/8
Kanban in sales	BT	6/8	

Projects

Parking Lot:

Plan:

Do:

Check:

Act:

Figure 3.2 Scrum Board.

indicates areas that are off course or are under threat of going out of control, and that need to be dealt with. The key with any red item is to quickly determine the root cause and identify the next steps to rectify these with actions or improvement projects.

It is this traffic light system, coupled with clear actions and projects that enables the rapid, typically stand-up meeting of 10–15 minutes. The stand-up nature of these meetings helps with the pace and keeping the alertness of team members. Once you have run rapid stand-up meetings for a time, you will know the difference instantly when you enter a traditional sit-down meeting. When people sit down, they naturally relax, talk more, sometimes drift off onto other things, which generally leads to an unproductive meeting. There is a fantastic ability for people to fill up the allotted hour or two hours. When you next leave an extensive sit-down meeting, review how much of the meeting delivered value and what portion of time was this value delivered in? I have found that more is achieved in a 10–15 minute, stand-up RVM than most traditional meetings I have sat through.

Agenda for an RVM

1. Culture/team building
   Celebrate and recognize excellent work in line with the company's mission and values. Develop a cultural approach to build teamwork that suits your team.
2. Actions and project progress since last meeting
   If an action/project is overdue, or in threat of becoming overdue or off course, the owner of the specific action/project will discuss it.
3. Measure progress
   Any red measure is discussed, finding the root cause for the failure and identifying action required to solve the issue.
4. Strategic projects and measures
   Review the projects that the team are focused on. Projects that are off track or at risk of becoming off track are discussed. The manager for these projects will outline the root cause of the issue, commit to the actions required to bring the project back under control as well as highlight any support they may require.
5. Any additional actions or improvement projects?
   Capture other actions or improvement ideas the team has before the meeting finishes.

If a considerable discussion develops at any stage between a few attendees of the RVM that is not relevant to the group, ask them to take the conversation offline after the RVM. This keeps the meeting moving and delivering value for everyone.

Teams will run rapid meetings at least weekly, but running them daily is better. More frequent meetings allow groups to focus on strategy once a week and the daily measures for the other days of the week. This alternation of focus speeds up the RVMs even more.

A visual board can be established simply using software technology available to us now such as Microsoft Teams and its related programs. Microsoft Teams enables a remote or local team to login to a central system that brings together programs to allow an RVM. Applications such as Power BI enable the development of useful visual data using the traffic light system. Other programs such as Microsoft Planner allow the creation of easy-to-use action lists and projects to assign accountability and timelines and visualize progress. With programs like Microsoft Teams, local presence is not necessary. Team members can call in via their smartphones or laptops to view visual data and communicate as part of the RVM.

Culture Building in an RVM

There are many different culture-building approaches that teams can use, such as

1. Gratitude – Start the RVM with team members sharing something they are thankful for.
2. Snaps – Share an example of great teamwork since the last meeting. This sharing concludes with the team clicking their fingers. This originated from the film *Legally Blonde* (Luketic, 2001).
3. 3 H's – Team members share a hero, highlight, and hardship of theirs. This vulnerability builds greater understanding and empathy within a team. This originated from the Richmond Football Club (Shmook, 2017).
4. Stretches/warm-ups – The team stretches and warms up!
5. The marketing team at Signet have a friendly basketball free-throw competition incorporated into their meetings, using a mini hoop and ball. The winner gets lunch bought for them.

It is best if the team chooses or creates the approach that they like for team building at the start of the Scrum/Huddle. If the team owns and believes in the approach, it will take hold and help build and sustain your team culture.

Example: Culture Building in an RVM

A great example of an organization focused on culture is the Winson Group. "The Winson Way," as they call it, combines the organization's purpose, values and behaviors, and strategic execution approach. Winson Group's purpose is "Helping Australia Compete," which is about improving every day to help their customers compete. Their values are honor, ownership, and commitment, change for strength, and diligence (Figure 3.3).

Under these values, teams have defined key behaviors they would and wouldn't see if they were living their culture. This approach makes it very simple for team members to know if culture is being lived as an individual or a team. Many Winson Group teams start their RVM with what they call a "Winson Way" moment. This involves a team member sharing an example of another person or team really living the company's purpose and culture. The approach keeps this critical focus for the organization front of mind and helps the organization's culture improve consistently.

Winson Group's teams understand the effort required to change behavior. They know it is not a quick process. If they define a critical behavioral area

Figure 3.3   Winson Group's Values and Behavior.

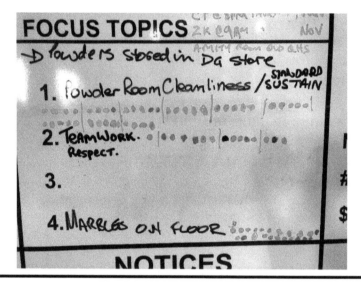

Figure 3.4 Team Behavior Change Tracker.

that they need to improve upon, they will track performance in this area over many weeks and months, depending on the complexity of the change.

Example: Daily Tracking of Habit Change

Figure 3.4 shows a sample from the organization's ink division led by Paul Hughes. This chart tracks the daily performance of the new behavior the team is looking to form into a habit. Good days are noted with a green dot and bad days with a red dot, which drives actions to keep effort on track. This whole process is owned and led by the front-line team.

Strategy Execution in an RVM

An annual strategic plan is usually formed by senior executives and then executed through a monthly review system. We have already covered the concept of Hoshin Kanri and Catch Ball (Dennis, 1982) to deploy strategy down to all levels of the organization in a way that creates empowerment, energy, and accountability. Strategy is all about change. What do we need to do differently to sustain or create a competitive advantage into the future? I don't know of any changes that can be achieved with only a monthly meeting, which equates to only 12 conversations a year. The RVM approach enables change to occur with constant focus, effort, and much discussion.

Once you reach middle and front-line teams, the strategy is about clear behaviors, actions, projects, and measures. Measures are a vital aspect of strategy that can be overlooked. We have already covered the difference between lead and lag measures. I propose that the more leading a strategic measure of focus can be for a team, the better. The other factor is to not focus on too many strategic measures. What are the two or three key improvement steps you can track and drive, which will bring you the highest decisive result?

Trend-Line Chart

A great tool to track this is a trend-line chart, also called a burn-up or burn-down chart (depending on the improvement path of the trend line). A burn chart enables a team to trend a target over time, which will ultimately lead to strategic success. Over time, team members can track their own performance against this measure, again driving actions and projects to achieve the targets. This chart uses the traffic light concept of red and green with a black line or dots to track the performance. The top section is green, and the bottom section is red as it is a burn-up chart with success lying on the upward trend. These charts are also often called watermelon charts (Figure 3.5).

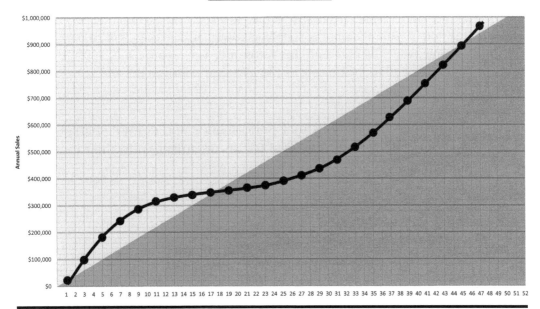

Figure 3.5   Burn-Up Watermelon Chart.

Action Orientation in an RVM

The main focus of RVMs is performance and building forward momentum. Actions and improvement projects with clear ownership and timelines are critical to developing a performance culture. Empowerment always precedes accountability, and for this reason, the person who owns the action or project needs to specify the timeline they will deliver it within. After this, they are fully responsible for the delivery of the outcome. For slight improvements or issue resolutions, which will take up to a week, a simple action list may be all that is required to track and manage the commitment. A great example of a performance huddle with effective action tracking can be found at Ingham's Pty Ltd Australia.

> **Example: Ingham's Action List**
>
> Ingham's, one of Australia's largest food processors, has implemented a high quality visual board as part of their RVM (Figure 3.6). The graphs and data have been shaded out for confidentiality reasons, but an essential aspect of their board is the action list, which can be seen in Figure 3.7.
>
> Joe Mientjes, the Production Manager at Ingham's, established this action list, which firstly splits short-term and long-term actions. This is important, as team members seeing an extensive list of slow-moving actions will often lose interest. By dividing the tasks, team members can expect to see the long-term actions stay on the board for longer with minimal change.
>
> The ingenuity of Joe's action list is the "Revised Date" section. For a failed action, a team member is simply asked what date they will deliver the outcome, which is noted on this list in red. This approach is a subtle enough reprimand to kick most people into gear with respect and accountability.

It is through many conversations that performance and culture change are achieved. The RVM approach is pivotal for an organization in their journey toward achieving excellence.

Suggested Actions for Scrum

1. Review as a team the results of your actions from the Hoshin Kanri section (Chapter 2) of this book.
2. Choose a team to start practicing the RVM concept. It is best to start at the executive level and then cascade the process to middle management

Figure 3.6   Ingham's Daily Operations Review Board.

SHORT TERM ACTIONS				
Date	Issue/Action	WHO	Due Date	Revised date
LONG TERM ACTIONS				
Date	Issue/Action	WHO	Due Date	Revised date

Figure 3.7 Ingham's Action List.

and then to front-line teams. This enables leaders to become skilled before they try and deploy the process with their teams.

3. Create a visual trend-line watermelon chart for each key strategic measure, ensuring they drive improvement over time for the lag measures of focus.
4. Define the day-to-day measures or key performance indicators (KPIs) that need to be sustained to ensure value is delivered to both your internal and external customers. Develop a traffic light system for these on your board.
5. Develop an action list.
6. Find a blank section of the wall, and mount your Hoshin Kanri plan, the watermelon charts, day job measures, and action list templates.
7. Set a daily, multi-time a week, or weekly time of 10–15 minutes for your RVMs, and follow the agenda previously mentioned.
8. Integrate the next section on Kanban into your meeting at the right time to more effectively manage projects and significant improvements.

Chapter 4

Agile Sales Concept 4: Kanban

The word "Kanban" (meaning signboard or billboard in English) and its model used in production are credited to Taiichi Ohno of Toyota and are a vital part of the Toyota Production System (TPS). Ohno is thought to have discovered the process in the late 1940s by studying supermarket stocking systems. The supermarkets Ohno saw were using a visual min–max inventory system for managing shelf stock. This simple process eliminated stock-outs and minimized stock wastage in these supermarkets which were seen as critical factors in customer satisfaction.

Toyota and many manufacturers since have used a Kanban system to create a visual min–max style inventory system for every aspect of the production process from raw material storage, work in progress, and parts through to finished goods. The basis of Kanban is creating an even flow of inventory through a process using a visual minimum and maximum stocking level. This enables a human or electronic system to instantly react when demand drops the stock level below the minimum level.

The primary benefit of Kanban within a factory is that the visual system manages inventory levels, not stocking too much and restocking only when needed. Kanban, when set up well, creates a flow of production that aligns with customer demand. It is called a pull system, as customer demand pulls inventory through the system rather than production pushing out as much stock as it can. The method avoids overburdening people and machines by evening out the workload and, in doing so, produces higher efficiency and performance.

Figure 4.1 shows a quality Kanban system setup in a factory scenario. There are two items of inventory between each workstation. When a

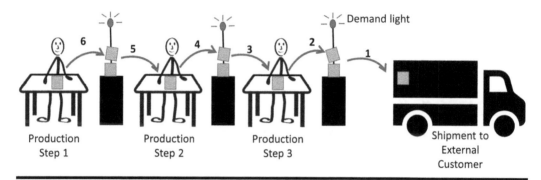

Figure 4.1   Quality Kanban Flow.

customer places an order, and an item is picked and shipped, the inventory in the final stock station reduces below two. This triggers a demand light prompting the operator at production step 3 to restock the station to their left with one item and then take the work in progress item from the station to their right. This triggers the same pull of demand back down the production line in a chain reaction. The efficiency of this system is impressive. I have seen cases where four times the productivity is achieved, with team members seeming to work less strenuously by implementing a Kanban system.

The reason for better performance is that a Kanban system running well avoids this push-based system (Figure 4.2).

In the push-based system, a large batch of work is building up at production step 2. Step 1 keeps producing, putting more pressure on step 2. Work is being pushed through the process in a large batch. This leads to overburden at production step 2, which leads to stress, time delays, and mistakes. Meanwhile, further down the production process in step 3, the process has stopped. The result of this occurrence is the underutilization of resources

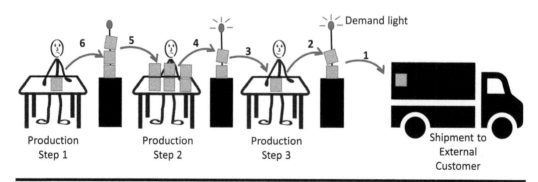

Figure 4.2   Push-Based Production System Overburdened.

and long delays before the product reaches the customer. Once a product does get past production step 2, it still needs to get through step 3 before it is finally ready to be sent to a customer.

The unfortunate factor is that humans typically think and operate in a batch push-based approach (Figure 4.2) rather than establishing a pull-based system with consistent flow (Figure 4.1). Another disappointing factor is that this is found to occur in project management and sales opportunity pipeline management. We focus on a batch of sales opportunities or a batch of improvement projects and work hard to succeed with them. At some stage, we look back at our opportunity or project list and think to ourselves, "Oh no, I am going to have nothing to move forward with." We rapidly start finding some more leads/project ideas quickly, but it is too late to avoid some quiet sales periods. This behavior leads to the same outcomes we explored within the push-based factory example.

When sales teams batch opportunities and become overburdened with them, they stop bringing new leads and prospects into the sales pipeline. Figure 4.3 shows a typical sales process in the form of an opportunity pipeline.

The salesperson is overburdened. All of their deals are sitting at the "negotiate" and "close" steps. They are so busy and flat out with this glut of sales closing that they have entirely neglected to "research" and "quote" on new deals. The pipeline has become blocked. When the salesperson finally reacts to this situation, a large gap of emptiness has occurred within the

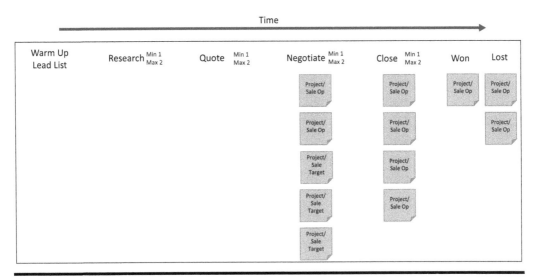

Figure 4.3   Sales Pipeline.

vital steps of "warm-up," "research," and "quote." This emptiness represents a period when deals are not being won. The overburden of the batch-style approach leads to less satisfactory sales performance. Salespeople start rushing, getting stressed, and not performing as well as they usually would. This leads to a poor win–loss ratio and less revenue.

Figure 4.4 shows a quality pull-based sales pipeline using an effective Kanban system. This approach works very well with marketing and sales teams collaborating on a lead generation system that generates leads in line with the sales pipeline empty gaps/requirements. The focus of this pipeline is to create a cadence of deal management that is paced with the cycle time of opportunities and closing rate the salesperson is achieving (pull-based system). To achieve a similar sales pipeline, each salesperson needs to have a visual Kanban opportunity pipeline with regular RVMs and one-on-ones occurring within their team and with their leader, respectively. It is essential that a cross-functional management RVM is happening at the level above them to ensure marketing is across the pipeline and pacing their work on lead generation in line with this. The visual nature of the Kanban allows Agile decisions to be made to keep the pipeline healthy, overcoming blockages and taking steps to keep an even flow.

A salesperson with a pull-based Kanban opportunity pipeline will not be overburdened. They will be in a state of flow, performing at their best. This means greater success, a better win–loss ratio, and more sales. The salesperson and team as a whole will not end up with periods of poor sales due

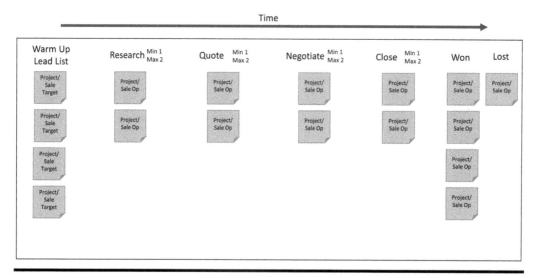

Figure 4.4   Pull-Bases Sales Opportunity Pipeline Using Kanban Approach.

to opportunity pipelines blocking or emptying at any stage of the process. With a full opportunity pipeline, deals are regularly completed, bringing consistent sales performance. A steady opportunity pipeline also provides a far greater chance of deals being won, as the salesperson will be less stressed and pressured.

I was listening to a fantastic podcast called the Advanced Selling Podcast (Caskey, 2019). Well-done hosts Bill Caskey and Brian Neal! Bryan mentioned a diagram (Figure 4.5) that highlights the need for an effective Kanban opportunity system.

This diagram indicates that the highest level of sales performance occurs with a medium level of workload and pressure. I can relate to this. When I have a good volume of work, I am in the zone, able to achieve great things. If a spike in work occurs, I can quickly be thrown into overburden, and the quality of my work drops. The same happens with salespeople; they can be in the zone of high performance and quickly slip into the high-pressure area, and their performance falls.

Bryan made an interesting point during the conversation. He mentioned that people who enter the area of high pressure and low performance experience so much pressure that it is hard for them to simply move back into the high-performance zone. Typically, they initially move to a position of low work and low pressure (chill out for a while) before they can get themselves back to the sweet spot of medium stress and workload. He stated it is a cyclical phenomenon.

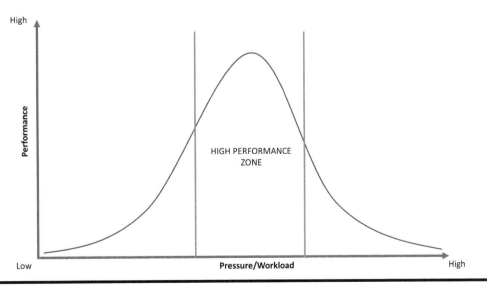

Figure 4.5   Sales Performance Bell Curve.

The Kanban approach to sales pipeline management, coupled with a quality approach to RVMs and one-on-ones, avoids these situations occurring. The systems help a team monitor their stress levels and put in place actions to keep everyone in the sweet spot of high performance with an even, full opportunity pipeline.

You could consider incorporating the sales performance bell curve into your RVM and ask team members to plot their current position before starting the RVM. This approach can lead to team members supporting each other to sustain everyone in the high-performance zone.

Setting Up a Kanban Board for Sales Opportunities and Improvement Ideas

Before setting up a Kanban board, you need to have a process or sales framework that your team agrees upon and are committed to following. This sales process becomes the basis of the Kanban. Most Customer Relationship Management (CRM) packages come with a standard sales flow, typically covering stages like "lead," "qualify," "develop," "propose," and "close." We will explore creating your own value-added approach based on Agile Sales concepts further on in this book. If you are looking to implement an improvement Kanban as part of your RVM, you could use the standard Sprint concept. We will cover Sprint using Plan, Do, Check, Act (PDCA) in the next chapter.

Once you have the stages defined for your Kanbans, the next step is to determine what the right medium for you to display them is. This question really comes down to, "What is the right medium to run your RVMs in?" For a team that is locally based and does not have a quality CRM or reporting technology, a manual board mounted on the wall does a great job. Simply design your board to cover the elements previously mentioned for an RVM, and include lanes for your Kanbans. Post-it notes are a simple tool that you can use to capture sales opportunities and quickly move them through the Kanban (Figure 4.6).

If you are lucky enough to have CRM software such as Salesforce, you will be able to set up an electronic RVM and Kanban. Salesforce planned ahead in their program design and was one of the firsts to incorporate a sales opportunity pipeline Kanban feature into its software (Figure 4.7). This feature has enabled sales and marketing teams all over the world to gain better visualization of their pipeline health rapidly. It has saved vast

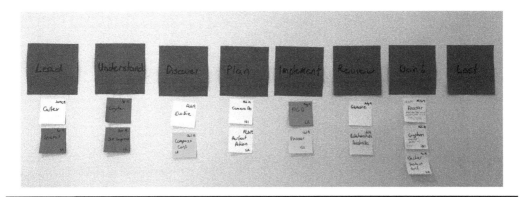

Figure 4.6   Sales Opportunity Kanban Using Post-Its.

amounts of time for salespeople who can simply drag and drop opportunities across new stages of the sales process as they progress.

Most importantly, it has enabled salespeople to remain in the high-performance zone (Figure 4.5). It helps them sustain a full opportunity pipeline that minimizes spikes of either too many or too few opportunities at any stage of the pipeline. The result is higher performance and more sales which everyone loves! If your organization is willing to invest in a large touchscreen TV/display, you can conduct your RVM around this. Drag and drop the opportunities; interact with measures, actions, and other vital elements. The Kanban system also provides a great focal point for one-on-one meetings. These can be conducted around a smartboard together, or remotely, as the data is all there and the technology available for remote connection.

My recommendation is to make a start, anywhere, and improve from there. You may not be able to go straight to a program like Salesforce. Start with some form of Kanban approach, grow your sales, and then invest at the right time to improve further.

Determining Kanban Capacity/Volume

What is the right capacity to have in your Kanban system? What are the correct minimum and maximum number of opportunities to have at each stage of the Kanban? The quick answer is that the system is dynamic; you don't set a level and stick with it forever. As a sales team, you will run improvement Sprints to improve your own processes, save time and enable salespeople to focus on delivering more value to customers. (In Agile, these are called Retrospectives, where a team is reviewing their own processes and running rapid improvements on them.) In this scenario, you will increase

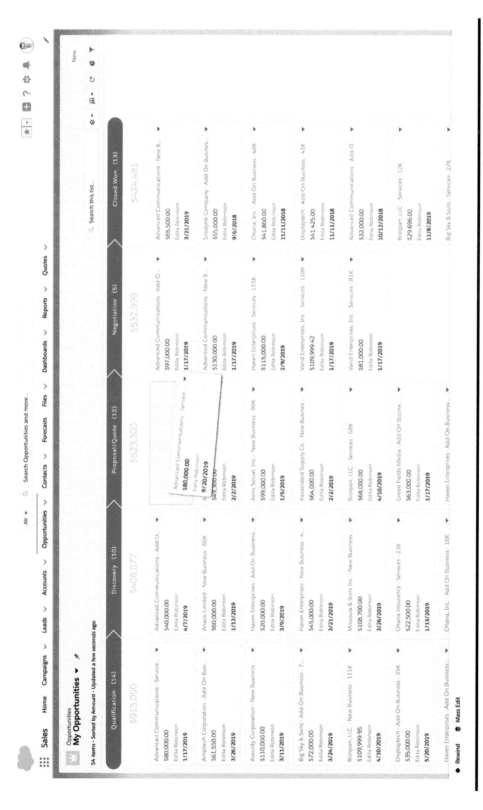

Figure 4.7 Salesforce CRM Opportunity Kanban.

the volume of projects in the Kanban or choose to work to manage opportunities through more quickly.

The other instance which could arise is that a salesperson's pipeline may become full of more substantial and complex sales opportunities. The salesperson may choose to reduce the volume of projects in the Kanban pipeline for some time while they focus on the more significant opportunities. The key with any Kanban system is to keep it full and moving without bottlenecks and the build-up of breaks at any one stage.

When first establishing a sales opportunity Kanban, a great way to determine the initial volume of the Kanban is to capture the following three measures:

1. The number of opportunities a salesperson has won in the last 12 months,
2. The conversion rate for the opportunities, and
3. The average cycle time or time from lead to closing the opportunities.

An example of this formula is

1. 60 opportunities won in the last 12 months,
2. 50% conversion rate, and
3. Average cycle time of two months.

Using this data, you can calculate the volume of opportunities in the Kanban at any one time and from this set a min–max volume:

(60 won opportunities/50% conversion) ÷ (12 months in a year/ two-month average sales cycle time)

= 20

You then divide the result by the number of stages in your sales process leading up to a deal closing. If you have four stages in your sales process, the result would be five. You would have a max level of five and set a minimum of three. You would also track the average cycle time to ensure it does not increase from two months.

You now have the structure for your Kanban sales pipelines. If you refer to the previous Salesforce CRM image (Figure 4.7), the min–max in this Kanban could be eight min–twelve max. You can see in the picture that the Kanban is over volume at the "qualification" stage and under at "negotiation." The "negotiation" stage is actually quite a large way down, showing only five opportunities. This would be the focus area in this case; working more deals with the "negotiating" stage while keeping the other steps in the opportunity Kanban full.

As I mentioned earlier, the key is to establish a starting point and evolve from there. Moving to a Kanban system will improve your team's productivity and sales output purely through eliminating the potential for overburdening or empty sales pipelines. This will enable your team to either bring deals through the sales cycle more quickly or increase the Kanban volume. Please note it is important not to increase the Kanban to a scale that creates overburdening of your sales team, taking them out of the high-performance zone (Figure 4.5). Equally important is to avoid making it too small and dropping your sales team into the underutilization stage of low performance.

I have mentioned a few times that the Kanban concept can also be used for improvement projects. This concept is called Sprints and is the next key element of Agile that we will explore.

Suggested Actions for Kanban

1. Define the steps in your sales process as a team.
2. Determine pipeline volume (using formula) to set the min–max levels for your Kanban.
3. Create a visual board, either physical or electronic – many CRM systems have a Kanban charting tool built in.
4. Plot your current deals into the chart, and see if you have any spikes already. Do you have a batch of deals all sitting at the same stage in the process well over your max level? Also, check if you have any gaps in the pipeline where the number of deals sitting in any one stage is below your minimum.
5. Bring the Kanban process into your RVM. Be sure with Kanban to focus the conversation on the next steps to move deals forward and how to overcome any spikes or gaps.
6. Implement the sales performance bell curve into your RVM to keep track of team members who are finding themselves out of the high-performance zone. Help team members who drop out of the high-performance zone get back into it.

Chapter 5

Agile Sales Concept 5: Sprints

During the studies conducted by Nonaka and Takeuchi (Nonaka and Takeuchi, 1986) in Japan, they noticed an iterative, cross functional teamwork approach to product development. This was entirely different from the predominant Western approach to large projects which ran in a linear flow over a long period with stage gates. It was likely a demonstration of the Deming cycle, as developed by Edwards Deming following the World War II (Figure 5.1). Japanese businesses, as a whole, embraced Deming's scientific ideology.

This approach has become the backbone of continuous improvement within organizations in today's market. It is a straightforward process:

1. Plan
   Plan your next improvement step for your internal or external customer that will help you move toward your future vision or objective.

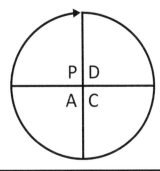

Figure 5.1   Deming Cycle.

Define a measure of success for the improvement step. Check-in with stakeholders, gather feedback, and adjust the approach if needed.

2. Do

Implement the improvement step, showing respect to everyone involved, keeping stakeholders informed.

3. Check

Check the outcome of the improvement step. Did you get the results you predicted in the Plan phase? Present the results back to stakeholders.

4. Act

Act on the results of your check. The check may result in further adjustments and movements again through improvement cycles to realize these. The Act phase may result in the updating of documentation and providing additional training because the Check phase was a success.

5. Plan

Plan your next improvement step and targeted outcomes, and move through the cycle again.

The Plan–Do–Check–Act (PDCA) cycle is a continuous cycle that is focused on iterative improvement. It is this approach that I believe played a large part in the branding of Agile. Naturally, organizations with a culture of scientific thinking (PDCA) will have a high level of agility.

I am a traditionalist and will stick with the PDCA cycle to define the concept of Sprint for sales teams. You can look up one of the many other approaches that have been established to outline scientific thinking.

Figure 5.2 shows the iterative, continuous improvement approach toward a vision or objective. Each cycle of improvement within Agile is called a Sprint. Sprints are typically small improvement steps that a team can engage in with high energy, generating data and achieving results quickly to learn from.

Traditionally, project management builds the perfect product before engaging the market. It takes a long time, costs a lot of money, and, when it does not succeed, fails miserably.

On the contrary, Agile is about

■ Focusing improvement on improving internal or external customer value and delight,
■ Having a vision or objective for the future,
■ Creating a theory or concept to move forward and test on (In Agile, this is called a User Story or an Epic for larger visionary improvement ideas.),

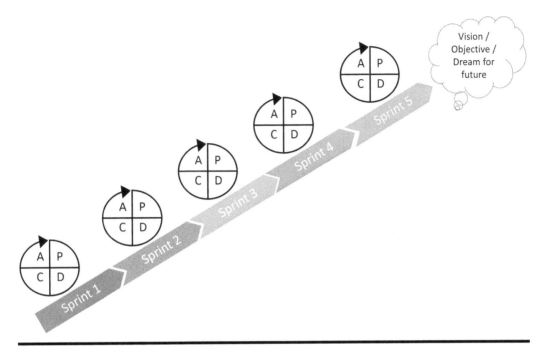

Figure 5.2   Sprint Cycles.

- Building the test product/idea quickly,
- Deploy the concept to a target customer or market segment,
- Check-in with the target customers to gain feedback,
- Monitoring and learning from critical leading customer behavioral measures that can predict long-term success,
- Learning and improving from these measures and direct customer feedback,
- Updating documentation,
- Engaging stakeholders, and
- Entering another improvement cycle to experiment further and learn again.

Agile uses the RVM to collaborate and conduct the Sprint approach.

Sprints in Sales

I have been fortunate to work with sales and marketing teams that have a culture of continuous improvement. This culture is not formed purely by implementing the Sprint concept. It requires all seven Agile concepts to truly achieve great things. The team needs to know who their ideal customers and personas are and what they value and gain delight from. They have used this data during their Hoshin Kanri process, and from this, they have a clear plan, mission, and vision for the future. They have an RVM forum to collaborate and run improvement Sprints. They can then work together using the Sprint concept to run rapid experiments to innovate for customers. They conduct these experiments in a targeted way, using measures and direct customer feedback to learn and experiment/improve further from.

Sales and marketing teams can use the Sprint approach to iteratively improve a new sales or marketing approach. They can also use the Sprint concept to eliminate waste out of their teams creating more time to deliver value to customers. This internal process improvement approach in Agile starts with a regular "Retrospective," a process where the team reflects on their current processes and define the most important areas to improve now. Waste, in Agile terms, is anything you do that a customer does not really care about and would not pay you money to do. Value is anything a customer would pay you to do. This does not have to be a physical product; it could be gaining knowledge or insight through a sales meeting.

I have facilitated many waste and value analysis events with sales teams (Retrospectives). We always come back to the same result – the only time that you deliver value in sales and marketing is when you engage a customer. For sales, this could be the moment a customer gains insight or knowledge from you, via email, in a face-to-face meeting, or over the phone.

The largest waste areas in sales are typically time related:

■ Driving time
■ Time preparing proposals or quotes
■ Time trying to get people on the phone and set meetings
■ Time trying to collate data, reports or find information they need

Customers don't care about these things; they certainly would not pay you money for these actions. Agile sales teams are regularly running Retrospectives to reflect on their processes and where they need to improve. They are running Sprints during their RVMs to win the war on waste: to continuously improve and innovate to minimize and eliminate those "non-value" actions, so that they can spend more time on the things customers will pay for. The natural result of this war on waste is more sales!

Innovation in sales and marketing is significant as it sustains a valuable point of difference for customers. Unfortunately, I have been called into many sales teams that have been doing the same thing over and over for many years. Ultimately their competition has caught up and overtaken them, and they need help. It is in teams like this that you hear the classic statements of

1. That is the way it has always been done.
2. It worked in the past.
3. We tried that once, and it didn't work.

Teams who have grown accustomed to the status quo become stuck. They form habits doing the same thing over and over, and this becomes very comfortable for them. The Agile concepts, including Retrospectives and Sprints, can really help these teams get out of the quicksand of stagnant innovation and start moving forward again.

Implementing Sprints

If you have implemented the first four Agile concepts well, involving everyone, creating empowerment and accountability, you will be in a great place to apply scientific thinking and implement Sprints.

Where should you focus your energy with Sprints? This should have been defined through your Hoshin Kanri approach, and ongoing Retrospective review events you conduct as a team. In general, there are two broad areas of focus:

1. Internal processes and improvement to eliminate waste and allow more time for value-adding activities, and
2. External customer-facing innovation and improvement.

With both approaches, the Sprint concept is not about changing everything through one large project. Sprints are about targeted experiments to learn and then improve from again and again. Innovation in lead generation campaigns is a great example to discuss within a targeted Sprint approach.

Traditionally, a sales and marketing team generates a concept for a new campaign, develops it, and then forces it out to the whole market. This approach mirrors the traditional linear broad project approach. It is often risky, costly, and hard to learn from. Too many customers have been contacted, and it is challenging to obtain varied and accurate data from which to learn and improve.

A targeted approach using the Sprint concept would involve selecting a key persona or two from the same geographical region (town, state, etc.) to conduct the initial experiment. Sprints can be performed quickly to form up the targeted campaign. The most significant benefit of this approach is the focused data and feedback that can be obtained from these targeted customers. In a highly focused approach, Contextual Interviews can be conducted with personas to gain input, which can then be used for the next Sprint improvement cycle. This is at the heart of the Agile approach: start small, experiment, learn, and then expand from there.

Example: Innovative Customer Improvement Using Sprints

A great example of innovative customer improvement comes from Signet. Signet had an objective to sell additional range into more customers. They measured this through "share of wallet." An idea for sales innovation was highlighted by a team member who had read a report based on the cost of having a multitude of suppliers rather than a consolidated few. The team thought of an innovative idea to provide insights to customers based on the costs of having multiple suppliers versus a single consolidated supplier. They developed critical data to support this concept and formed a process to take customers through a journey to consolidate supply, of course, through their own company, Signet.

Their initial Sprint was focused on developing these insights and providing the data to back them up. Their second Sprint focused on creating a few tools to help them record a customer's current purchasing habits and develop a proposed future state to deliver gains.

Both Sprint cycles were completed within a week. The third improvement cycle was focused on engaging a target customer with the new process. The team launched the approach with one customer in one territory only, finding amazing results very quickly. This experiment resulted in over one million dollars in new business, which was an astonishing result! The team has continued to run many subsequent Sprints on this area of innovation and are now broadening their approach to more wide-reaching regions. They are focused on leading customer behavioral indicators based on their sales process which is aligned to the customer buying journey. These lead indicators combined with direct customer feedback help them constantly reflect and learn between sprints.

The power of the Sprint is its attention to learning. This provides for rapid innovation and improvement that can't be achieved through large projects conducted in a linear approach over a vast territory.

When running the Sprint approach, a visual Kanban that allows you to effectively lead and manage improvements your team is working on is vital. Like an opportunity pipeline Kanban, best practice is to sustain a full and even Kanban for improvement projects. Overburden and bottlenecks will impact a team's performance with Sprints the same way it does with sales opportunities. Gaps or emptiness within your improvement Kanban will result in less growth achieved by the organization. It can also result in a lack of energy, focus, and interest being applied to Sprints and critical skills and habits not being developed. Additional data such as conversion rates and time between Kanban stages can also be monitored and used for learning and improvement ongoing.

Next, determine the Sprint cycle time (time to run PDCA) your team wants to focus on. This is typically a week, two weeks, or a month at the most. Improvement projects are then structured and sized with a focus on achievement within this cycle time.

The structure that I like for a Sprint Kanban is shown in Figure 5.3. Again, this Kanban would become part of the RVM and can be developed manually or electronically using programs such as MS Planner. When considering how often to review your Sprint Kanban as part of your RVM, consider the cycle time for your Sprints. A team running an improvement Sprint with a cycle time of one week will require a review multiple times a week. If your Sprint cycle time is one month, you will only need to consider this

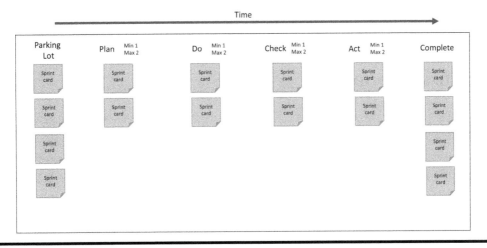

Figure 5.3 Sprint Kanban.

> **Sprint Card**
>
> **Sprint Name:** Delight Customer
> **Sprint Lead:** John Doe
> **Target Date:** ??/??/??
>
> **Current State:** (What is currently happening)
> **Future State Target:** (What do you want to be happening after the sprint and what is the measure of success?)

Figure 5.4 Sprint Kanban Card.

Kanban weekly. Please remember that RVM agendas can vary throughout the week or month to enable rapid meetings to sustain the meeting time of 10–15 minutes.

The final aspect to consider when implementing a Sprint is the Sprint card that you wish to use as part of this Kanban. Figure 5.4 shows a simple example of a Sprint Kanban card which captures the essential data you require to rapidly manage a Sprint. Ideas need to be customer centric and focused. In Agile, they are called "user stories" or "epics" for larger ideas. At a base level, a Sprint Kanban card needs to have a name, define a lead for the Sprint, and a completion date based on the standard sprint cycle time of focus. When setting the target, firstly identify the current state or problem you are dealing with. Then define on the card the future state and related measure of success you are looking to achieve through this Sprint. This simple approach allows you to clearly establish what is occurring currently that is leading you to run this Sprint and what you want to be happening in the future.

Prioritizing Sprints

As I have previously mentioned, overburden and bottlenecks with any Kanban system will really hurt the approach. When teams first begin a Sprint approach, the ideas for improvement come quick and fast (user stories or Epics). Soon a team finds itself overburdened with improvement ideas, and very few are achieved. Team members who raised ideas get annoyed because their thoughts went unnoticed, and no action resulted.

The Parking Lot (Figure 5.3) is one system to help control the number of improvements that enter the Sprint Kanban. Ideas can be placed within the

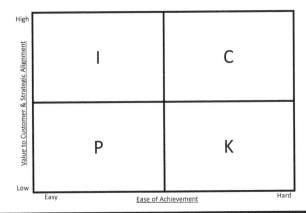

Figure 5.5 PICK Chart.

Parking Lot and assigned to a Sprint leader in line with the flow of the Kanban. Too many improvement ideas may still build up in the parking lot, leading to overburden. In this case, improvement ideas should be prioritized.

A great tool that can help a team prioritize improvement ideas together is the PICK chart (Figure 5.5). The emphasis is on working together as a team, not just the leader acting.

The PICK chart is a simple priority matrix. It allows an organization to review improvement ideas against the following criteria:

1. How easy are they to achieve?
2. What is the value to the customer?
3. What is the strategic alignment from the improvement?

Depending on the ranking of the improvement idea, it will fall into either the P, I, C, or K region of the chart. The associated words for P, I, C, K (possible, implement, challenge, and kill) provides the following recommendation of priority.

P = Possible. This improvement is easy to achieve but will provide low value to your customer and strategic focus areas for your team.

I = Implement. This improvement is easy to achieve and will provide high value to your customer and strategic focus areas for your team.

C = Challenge. This improvement is of high value but is difficult to achieve. You would typically prioritize improvements falling in the P and I sectors first, especially if you are just starting out on your continuous improvement journey. It is better to get a few easy wins for the team first to help build energy and confidence.

K = Kill. This improvement is of low value and difficult to achieve. Improvement ideas falling in this section would not be implemented.

The PICK chart provides a simple analysis system to enable a team to review new improvement ideas and existing improvement ideas within the Kanban if it becomes overburdened.

Sprints for Challenging Opportunities and Out-of-Control Kanbans

The Agile Sprint approach can overcome challenges in opportunities and reign in out-of-control Kanbans, just as easy as reducing waste and improving innovative thinking.

The first step with any problematic situation is to understand the root cause. When something goes amiss, we typically only see the symptom/result of what happened. There are always several inputs that lead to an opportunity stalling or a salesperson's opportunity pipeline becoming unmanageable. It is vital to be able to deeply understand this rather than just dealing with the result. This approach to deeply understanding a problem before you try and fix it (fix forever needs to be the goal) is called Root Cause Analysis.

There are many techniques for conducting Root Cause Analysis. I am going to cover the most straightforward approach, which is called the 5 Whys. The 5 Whys approach, which can be seen in Figure 5.6, merely asks "Why?" or "What caused a situation?" many times. Five times is only a guide; the key is to keep asking the question until the root cause found is unable

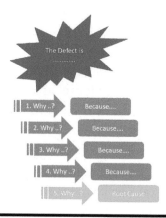

Figure 5.6   5 Whys Root Cause Analysis.

to be resolved and is outside of your control. Essentially, you begin with the defect or failure that has occurred and ask why this happened or what caused it. ("What" is a softer word than "why" that you can also use.)

Once you have a deeper understanding of the factors that caused a failure, you are in a much stronger position to run a Sprint to address the issue. Ideally, through improvement, you prevent it from occurring again. When conducting Sprints on challenges with opportunities or out of control opportunity pipelines, the same PDCA cycle applies. Part of planning is to ask the 5 Whys to understand the problem deeply. From the root cause findings, plan an improvement approach, and then complete the improvement. After a period, check the results, and then act based upon the findings. The action taken from the results could be to move quickly into another phase of experimentation if the check was not positive. If the check was positive, the response would be to sustain this improvement and ensure the issue does not arise again. A crucial part of maintaining gains from problems and issues or innovations that are moving an organization forward is leadership. Within Agile concept 6, we will review the critical part that leadership plays in sustaining an Agile journey.

In conclusion, it is essential to realize that the Agile Sales systems you develop and put in place will, at times, struggle. Don't lose heart with this; it only means you have a challenge that you need to overcome. The Root Cause Analysis and Sprint approach will help get your journey back on track. Reaching out for help when you need it is so important. The whole Continuous Improvement industry is full of people willing to share and help.

I have not experienced a more humble, accommodating industry in my career.

Suggested Actions for Sprints

1. Read further on scientific thinking. It is critical to break traditional project thinking and move toward customer-focused iterative experimentation.
2. Develop a Sprint Kanban board as part of your RVM together with a simple Sprint card.
3. Develop a standard time for your team to conduct a Retrospective, which could be linked to a regular RVM. Conduct a review of how your key processes are performing. During these events brainstorm where

improvement could be focused to achieve the greatest results quickly for customers.

4. Practice running some Sprints as a team using the PDCA approach.
5. Practice using the 5 Whys with an issue or problem that arises. Get to a deeper understanding of the problem through this process, and then conduct a few Sprint cycles if needed to prevent the problem from ever occurring again.

Chapter 6

Agile Sales Concept 6: Leader Standard Work

We have covered several Agile systems so far within this book, which, if run well, will help an organization improve rapidly into their future. The techniques will capture the minds and bodies of team members, but to be truly effective, an organization will also need to win their employees' hearts. The heart of an organization is its purpose/mission and culture. Without a focus on the heart, there will not be the energy, psychological safety and motivation to support long-term change.

We will explore the topic of culture and how to lead it throughout this chapter.

We have not yet spoken about culture extensively; however, it is imperative to your efforts to become more Agile. What is culture? To me, culture is a collection of mutual beliefs, attitudes, and behaviors that a connected group of people share. There will be existing behaviors and beliefs within your team that will help you implement Agile. There will also be elements of your existing culture that are hindering your efforts.

We are all creatures of habit. We are comfortable doing what we have always done because we know how to do it, are good at it, and have been successful and recognized for it in the past. I am confident that we can all think of people we have tried to convince to do something differently without success. The barriers to change can be massive. This is not the case with all people. I like to refer to the Pareto Principle when analyzing tendencies of a group of people to embrace change. With significant change, the top 20% of people will embrace change with energy. The middle 60% will sit

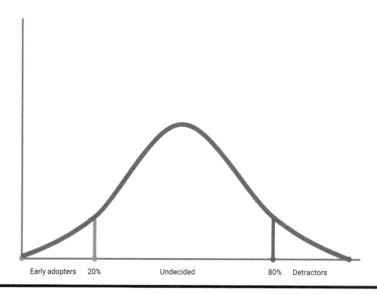

Figure 6.1 Change Pareto Principle Bell Curve.

on the fence and wait, and the bottom 20% of detractors will actively resist change. The volume of people at each stage looks like a bell curve; the middle mass is the largest group (Figure 6.1).

This ratio will vary greatly depending on the size of the upcoming change. A small alteration will not see the Pareto style split; you will have more early adopters and less detractors. The initial insight here is that people will handle taking small steps toward significant change, rather than having to accept large-scale change. Plan–Do–Check–Act (PDCA) Sprint thinking and making many small improvement steps is recommended if you are not in crisis and needing rapid large-scale change.

The bell curve figure shows that a large amount of work is required to bring the middle "undecided" through the journey. It is even more work to bring the "detractors" along. Whose job is it to lead such an effort, apply the constant energy to help people form the new habits required? Ultimately, it is the job of the leader of these people, supported by the informal leaders who are part of the early adopter group.

Leading Change

Changing human habits is not a simple task. If you wish to implement the Agile concepts we have covered so far, you will be

- Asking team members to put more time into understanding their customers,
- Involving everyone in strategic planning and deployment,
- Running rapid visual meetings (RVMs) that are focused on culture and performance,
- Running sales opportunities and improvement ideas through a project Kanban, and
- Using the Sprint iterative approach to achieve these improvements.

I am sure there will be some dramatic changes required to implement these concepts.

Think about a significant change you have tried to implement in your life: quitting smoking, breaking a habitual alcohol, coffee or junk food obsession, or exercising regularly. It is not easy, and it can take a long time before the new habit strengthens enough to resist the old comfortable practice.

Even when you think you have broken the old habit, something can trigger it to return again. With regular exercise, many of us will lean on a personal trainer or friend to help us sustain the effort of change and improvement. I believe the personal trainer within an organization is the leader and early adopters of the change. Leaders are positioned to support and apply constant energy long enough to see the change become part of organizational culture.

I have worked with many leaders who have asked me to train their people in a new skill with the assumption that once the training is complete, the job is done. Their attitude is that we have taught them, they now know what they need to do, and they just need to do it. This leadership attitude always leads to failure. Most humans can't change that quickly. We need constant energy over a long period to pick up new skills and form new habits. It is tough for leaders operating in today's fast-paced world to support the change long enough for it to sustain.

The starting point for any leader who is keen to improve their skills in leading change is to clearly define what is most important to focus on. The legend in the field of time management and leadership focus is Stephen Covey with his time management model and concept of putting the "first things first" (Covey, 1989). In Figure 6.2, I use his model to outline some key leadership behaviors which are detrimental to leading excellence and change. Note the critical section for effectiveness is in the *important/not urgent* (Q2) quadrant of the matrix.

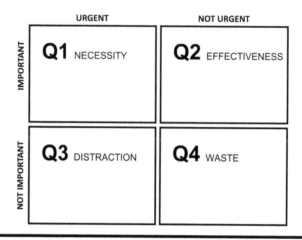

Figure 6.2   Time Management Matrix (Covey, 1989).

Leading change requires leaders to sustain constant energy on the change they are seeking, continually communicating, demonstrating, and supporting team members with the new behavior. These tasks are not urgent and can quickly become disrupted by "important/urgent" (Q1 necessity) and "not important/urgent" items (Q3 distraction). Leaders who get caught in the "urgent" can quickly find themselves not applying energy to important change supporting activities. Time can pass by quickly, and when the leader finally gets the chance to check back on the changes that had been implemented, they find them out of control and derailed. The key for a leader is to initiate the right time management system to help sustain their focus on the few *important/not urgent* items critical to the organizational journey.

Sustaining Constant Focus on *Important, Not Urgent*

The way that a leader can continue to give attention to leading change is not complicated, but it is not easy to maintain. Peter Hines and Chris Butterworth, in their award-winning book *The Essence of Excellence* (Hines and Butterworth, 2019), write about the concept of Leader Standard Work. They outline that Leader Standard Work is the way to sustain constant focus and support on the improvement and work on achieving organizational change and excellence.

Leader Standard Work requires a leader to define the few behaviors critical for them to continually adhere to, to maintain energy on what is most important. Leader Standard Work allows a leader to define new changes and initiatives that they need to check and support over a period to ensure the change succeeds.

Typical behaviors required of leaders to initiate change are

1. Attending RVMs,
2. Conducting one-on-ones with agenda items focused on team member development, strategy and change,
3. Spending time where fundamental changes have been implemented to review and support,
4. Proactively participating in project and strategy review meetings, and
5. Actively communicating and demonstrating new change behaviors in everything they do.

To stop the "urgent" items pushing these *important/not urgent* items aside, a leader needs to block out their time and diligently prohibit the urge to disrupt these essential items. The way a leader does this can look different depending on their role. Front-line leaders tend to use a physical Leader Standard Work form (Figure 6.3).

This form allows a leader to set daily and weekly time slots for important tasks in leading excellence. They can also note changes to monitor and challenges that arise and their root causes. The form is designed to be used either electronically or manually. Typically, when completed, this form will be passed to their leader as a communication tool.

Leader Standard Work for middle and senior leaders can be as simple as setting pre-defined meetings and blocking out times within their calendar or diaries. It is essential to consider adopting a precise method to capture the areas of change to monitor. This system also needs to capture any challenges which arise during Leader Standard Work.

Many of the challenges identified during Leader Standard Work will channel into the appropriate RVMs or one-on-one meetings for action. Leader Standard Work links simply into the other Agile systems we have covered. Leader Standard Work creates an aligned approach to leading excellence through creating a more nimble, Agile culture.

Key Skills for Conducting Effective Leader Standard Work

Blocking out time to perform the critical behaviors of Leader Standard Work is a good start. These behaviors include attending RVMs, walking front-line

Name: Role: Date:

Leader Standard Work						

Time	✓	Daily Tasks	Notes	Day	✓	Weekly Tasks
8:00				Mon		
9:00						
10:00				Tue		
11:00						
12:00				Wed		
13:00						
14:00				Thu		
15:00						
16:00				Fri		
18:00						
19:00						
20:00						

Changes to Monitor and Support Daily	✓	Key Measure

Challenges Identified and Root Cause

Figure 6.3   Front-Line Leader Standard Work Form.

areas, and monitoring change where it counts. It involves making sales calls with team members, visiting customers, conducting one-on-one meetings, and taking part in project and strategy review sessions.

The next aspect of leading excellence is what you do during these meetings and walks. There are four key areas of skill development which can help a leader enhance their performance and effectiveness at leading excellence. These are

1. Embracing early adopters,
2. Defining behaviors and leading them,
3. Creating the right environment, and
4. Continuously improving coaching skills.

Embracing Early Adopters

Early adopters are your greatest allies when leading change. They have embraced the change and are energized and ready to help. Early adopters are those people who sit outside of a store all night to be the first ones to buy a new product the next day. Why do they do this? They could get to the store that afternoon or the next day and still purchase the latest product. Early adopters want to be first, and they want to be recognized from their leader and from their peers for being first. Embracing early adopters and helping them shine is playing directly to their innate motivational nature. Through recognition, you will be giving them time in the spotlight while building a support network to help you bring the rest of the organization along on the ride.

Early adopters who have been embraced and recognized will become informal leaders, working side by side with you to help the change succeed. This is precisely what you need when working to achieve success with change. With substantial change, it is critical that leadership, together with the early adopters, focus on the middle masses, not the detractors. It is essential to withhold your attention from the detractors. Instead, focus all of your energy on the middle masses, encouraging them to join you on the journey. This process creates a chain reaction. As more and more people get onboard with the change, you acquire more and more advocates who will then also help you to succeed.

Example: Early Adopter

When I was first involved in organizational improvement, there was a young early adopter, Evan Powell who I embraced from an early stage on the change journey. Evan was in a junior role at the time and showed high energy toward adopting change to help the organization improve and grow. To recognize Evan's support and embrace him as part of the change, I was able to get him tickets to a two-day conference in his field of interest. I went to this event with Evan, got to know him more, and we both gained a lot of knowledge and some key contacts to help with the changes we were embarking upon. Since that time, Evan has had a significant role in supporting and motivating others in the excellence journey. His career has progressed now into senior leadership, placing him in a strong position to influence and support a wider group of people. Evan leads the best practices that we implemented. He has embraced and supported many early adopters, building on the catalyst created to establish what is now an Agile, high-performing culture of excellence.

Defining Behaviors and Leading Them

Many organizations have identified their core values and mounted these on the walls of their offices and operational areas. These displays often look great, but when you talk to employees, they see them as not much more than wall decorations. Culture is often seen as a mystical thing, something that is difficult to lead and control, and for this reason, most leaders don't give culture much time. Extensive research has been done on the topic of culture, it's importance, and how to effectively lead and improve it.

When you look at an organizational value, it can be tough to know if it is being lived. This would become a lot clearer if the said value included a definition of the critical behaviors (Hines and Butterworth, 2019) that you would see if it was being lived. Let's look at a typical organizational value – "agility." To achieve agility, an organization must have forums for team members to come together, focus, and drive improvement. A defined behavior may be "Team members show agility when they contribute improvement ideas at RVMs."

Another typical value is "respect." A defined behavior may be "Respect is demonstrated when leaders recognize employees for quality work during site walks." Everyone in the organization can see and hear leaders recognizing team members for great work and can link this recognition back to the company's core values. The other crucial factor is that these behaviors can be measured, tracked, and improved upon as a lead measure which you predict will ultimately enhance your culture.

This process may seem quite simple, which it is, but it is not easy. When you consider the change that you are looking to achieve, think to yourself, "How does this relate to organizational purpose and core values?" Ask your team, "What behaviors would we see if we were living our organizational purpose and values?"

These questions will lead you to a set of behaviors that you can see, measure, and lead. Traditionally, in business, we have focused on key performance indicators (KPIs). Considering the importance of a more Agile future state, behavioral measures will become even more imperative. If you actually define behaviors relating to your core values, you will be able to see if they are being lived. You will be able to measure them as key behavioral indicators (KBIs) (Hines and Butterworth, 2019) and track improvement in your culture through this. KBIs can form a part of Leader Standard Work templates and team RVMs to help motivate and drive the change required.

If you are serious about implementing Agile in your organization, we have already covered several key behaviors you will need to see. Don't be afraid to define these key behaviors and incorporate them into your RVM as visual measures or as KBIs and then recognized great performance in these behaviors. There is no better way of sustaining constant focus on them long enough to see the new habits form and improve.

Creating the Right Environment

Subconsciously, we are all highly influenced by the environment we live and work in. We are visual beings; so much of the information that we take into our brains enters through our eyes. What we see on any given day ultimately influences the way we feel, think, and then behave. Have you ever had to work in a dark or dirty office? How did this make you feel? Did it make you feel less energetic than usual, even less confident? Compare this to a time you have worked or spent time in a professional and clean environment? Did the environment make you feel more organized, energetic, and more qualified?

The workplace environment will also be impacted by the language and emotions being shown by others, especially the leaders. A workplace where the leader is angry, frantic, and unhappy will have a catalyst effect on others – they will feel the same negative emotions. Alternatively, a workplace where the leader is positive and energetic will have the opposite, uplifting effect.

Think about your ideal organizational culture. What behaviors and attitudes do you want your people to demonstrate? Then look at your workplace and the behaviors being shown and think, "How could we improve this environment to create our ideal culture?"

The essence of agility is that of energy and pace. To achieve energy and speed, you need an orderly workplace with visual data and information displayed allowing people to make decisions quickly. Agile is not about chaos; it is about focus and speed of innovation and improvement.

One particular Agile workplace comes to mind. The organization created a clean, professional environment with modern tables and plenty of greenery. The workplace had a mix of electronic screens and manual visual boards, showing critical day job and strategic metrics together with actions and project Kanbans. The workplace was also fun with high energy, created through fun elements such as gamification to celebrate achievements and peer-to-peer-recognition systems for high performance. The lunch area in this workplace was large and inviting; team members were motivated to take breaks, refuel, and recharge.

Agile is not achieved through constant full throttle workloads. To perform, humans require balance in their life, and balance comes through the work environment an employee engages with on a day-to-day basis.

Develop Your Coaching Skills

There are several languages that we can choose to use as a leader. We can choose to admonish someone, tell them with no uncertainty what they need to do and by when. We can try and sell a concept to someone and work to manipulate and persuade them to accept our views. Alternatively, we can ask people intelligent questions, drawing on their knowledge and getting them actively thinking in the process. Which approach would you prefer a leader to take with you?

There are times, mainly in safety situations, where admonishment may be required, but hopefully these are rare. Coaching is the skill of asking the right questions at the right time to encourage team members to think for themselves. Coaching is about motivating and developing others to reach their potential and succeed. In my mind, leading an organization is not very different from managing a sporting team. Both involve humans, and both are competitive situations and require agility, performance, and improvement.

Aligning Individual and Organization Goals

Coaching begins with the alignment of individual and organizational purpose and goals. If you can achieve this with an individual you have the basis for success. Whenever a leader comes to me with an issue with a staff member, I ask if they know their team members' purpose, goals, and motivations in life? 95% of the time, I draw a blank to this question. To start coaching someone, you need to know where they want to go, both personally and professionally. The more that these two align with the organization's direction, the more chance you have of high performance.

I was working with a team of salespeople a few weeks ago. We were exploring the organization's purpose, which was focused on helping customers improve for the betterment of their organization and the planet. I asked the team what this looks like and why it is essential? I got some great answers, capturing them on a flip chart as we went. They put forward ideas such as helping customers eliminate waste and reducing their carbon footprint through their products and services. When we had finished capturing all of their thoughts, I asked the team, "How much do these align with your own purpose and goals for the future?" Everyone in the group smiled. You could feel the positive energy in the room. This was a team working for an organization where their purposes and goals aligned. People working in this environment don't work a day in their life. Every day they get to wake up, live their purpose, and achieve their goals.

Asking the Right Questions

The next skill with coaching is asking the right questions at the right time to encourage people to think, grow, and learn for themselves. We are far more likely to adopt a skill that we have helped to develop, rather than an instruction we have simply been told. There is an old saying, "Tell me, and I forget, teach me, and I may remember, involve me, and I learn." If you tell someone something, you have a slim chance they will remember it after a few days. If you take some time and teach someone something, studies have found that 70% is forgotten one week later. If you involve someone in the discovery and challenge them to think and come up with the idea themselves, you have the highest chance of them remembering and adopting the new learning.

Involving someone and helping them learn for themselves requires a leader to use open probe questioning. These are questions that start with how, what, when, and why. Open probes are questions that make people think and answer in a sentence form. If an answer is OK, yes, or no, a closed probe has probably been used. Questions that can be answered with one word don't make people think profoundly and learn.

Consider the following example of questioning.

> "I need the report by 5 pm next Friday".
>   Or
>   "The report is due on Friday next week. How are you thinking about achieving this deadline? What support do you need?"

The second style of questioning has cost you maybe 30 more seconds, and the team member having to think and respond in a sentence may take another 30 seconds. I have found the extra time investment is well worth it, as it provides for a much higher improvement in results.

It is true, with some team members, you can simply tell them, and they will deliver. I have found that even with these team members, their performance improves by using open rather than closed probes, involving them and encouraging them to think. The majority of team members do not respond or deliver based on direct instructions without intensive follow-up and reminding. The level of follow-up and reminding decreases dramatically purely by asking open versus closed probe questions, involving team members, and encouraging them to think.

There are many coaching systems that you can study and learn from. I highly recommend that anyone study and practice coaching skills into their future. To me, it is one of the most essential skills to learn to help people and succeed, which ultimately benefits the organization. All of the coaching models I have studied promote the use of open probe questioning. All of them also follow a questioning formula like continuous improvement thinking, which I learned through my studies and time practicing Lean and Agile. The method of questioning follows a sequence as shown in Figure 6.4.

1. Future State
   What is your goal/objective with this situation? What do you want to achieve? What will the future look like? How will you know when you have achieved the objective? How important is it to you?
2. Current State
   What is happening now? What is occurring in this present moment that is making you want to move toward that future state? Why are these things occurring?
3. How?
   How will you achieve the future state? What options do you have in making it happen? What challenges and obstacles could arise that may impact achieving the goal? What is your best option to take?

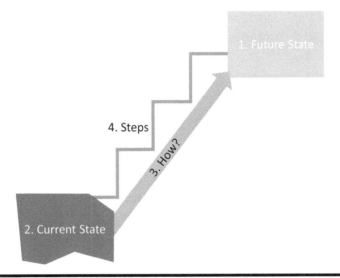

Figure 6.4 Coaching Process.

4. Steps

What steps are you going to take and by when to achieve the future state? What help will you need? Do you need help from anyone to achieve this? When do you need that help?

5. Review and support

How will we check back in to review progress and draw on further assistance if you need it?

I am sure this looks simple to you, as it has always seemed to me. Believe me, it is not easy to sustain. We all end up in situations where we are stressed, under time pressure, and just want to get things done! The best advice I can give you is to catch yourself when you feel this way, take a deep breath, and choose the coaching path rather than the "command and control" path. I have been practicing coaching for over 20 years. I still catch myself multiple times a day before I head into a "command and control" direct statement and actively choose the healthier path of coaching. It is not easy, and I have not been able to achieve a coaching approach as my natural habit yet. "Command and control" is still my natural go-to, mainly when I am tired, busy, and stressed.

A coaching approach works exceptionally well in your personal life as much as it does at work. I find my children, and especially my wife, respond to coaching language much more than direct orders and statements. The results I get are dramatically better using this approach rather than making direct closed command statements. If you figure out a way other than constant active thinking and practice to make this approach a natural habit, let me know.

You can contact me through my website www.iqi.com.au.

Storytelling

There is one final powerful coaching technique that has been around since mankind first learned to communicate. This approach has been used by many of the largest, most successful institutions over history to convey their messages. It is an approach we start using with our children from an early age, a method that we all respond to naturally. What I am referring to is storytelling.

Coaching using storytelling is being able to tell a short, clear story about the future that creates a vivid positive image in the other person's mind. This language approach is compelling as it taps directly into how our brain naturally learns. Think about the last time you read a book. Were you capturing the words in your mind, or were you painting a picture that related to the story you were reading? Our mind turns what we read into images to lock the information away, and the same applies in a powerful way with what we hear. If you adopt a storytelling approach to language, you are helping other people form an image and lock the information away in the ideal way (for their brain).

Successful stories are

- Short
  We all have a short attention span.
- Future oriented
  Our current state may be messy, but we love focusing on a positive future.
- Visually stimulating
  In your story, describe the future, how it looks, what we will feel, what we will hear.
- Achievable
  Don't exaggerate; make sure the future story is within peoples grasp.
- Motivational
  Tap into the purpose and goals of the organization and the people you are communicating to.

For many years, I have worked with a leader who is a fantastic orator, Jack Winson. When Jack stands up and makes a speech, everyone is glued to everything he is saying and come away feeling inspired. I now know that Jack is an excellent storyteller. His discussions and conversations are future focused. He describes the future, turns it into a picture, typically makes it achievable (sorry Jack, there have been some massive stretches sometimes), and creates motivation by tapping into the organization's and team members' purpose.

There have been some fantastic storytellers throughout history. Think of Martin Luther King's iconic speech, "I have a dream." One sentence from the speech states, "I have a dream that one day on the red hills of Georgia, sons of former slaves and the sons of former slave owners will be able to sit down together at the table of brotherhood" (King, 1963). Notice the motivational language (dream, brotherhood), the future orientation of this sentence, and the use of imagery (red hills, sitting together at the table). This was a truly inspiring speech and surely went a long way into shaping the climate for civil rights action in America.

When you have a goal that you want to communicate or a specific outcome, I recommend using storytelling rather than "command and control." It takes a bit more time to prepare for the conversation or speech, but the results will be dramatically better. You will be communicating with people in the way their minds want to be communicated with.

Suggested Actions for Leader Standard Work

If you are already a leader, aspiring to become a leader in the future, or an early adopter who likes helping your organization achieve great things, here are some suggested actions to take:

1. Note down what you have worked on for the last two to three days. Plot each item on the Stephen Covey time management chart.
2. Think about the *important/not urgent* things you could be doing. Capture the top three items on this list. What are the top three that would help your customers, your team, and yourself the most?
3. Think about how frequently you need to perform these, and set the time for them. Ask for help from a team member or leader to help keep focus on these and sustain the process.

4. What behaviors would you see yourself exhibiting each day or week if you were getting your *important/not urgent* activities done? How could you measure these as KBIs? How will you create a scoreboard for this and track performance?

5. Look at your work environment. Does it represent the future you want to be achieving, the culture you want to develop and sustain? How could you improve this?

6. Think about a way you could catch yourself before you use direct "command and control" language (this may be at home). How could you use open coaching language instead?

7. Find an opportunity to use storytelling in a conversation or during a speech or presentation you have coming up.

Next, we move into discovering the customer's buying journey and provide tips and tricks to help you engage with customers to deliver them higher value and delight in a structured way. We will explore ways to help you nail your sales results and have your name immortalized within your organization as one of the top gun achievers!

Chapter 7

Agile Sales Concept 7: Sales Process Aligned to Your Customer's Buying Journey

Customers are ultimately the ones who will influence, through their purchases, whether an organization succeeds or fails. How does a customer perceive your organization? What is the level of value and delight they encounter from interacting with your brand? Competitive advantage and success are realized when you can delight your customers, time and time again, earning their devotion.

Providing enlightening value to your customers requires processes that are continuously improved to sustain a unique point of difference. The logical way to build procedures and run improvements is to base them upon the journey a customer would like to experience rather than organizational preferences and opinions.

Figure 7.1 depicts a customer's buying journey and the multiple touch-points that customers receive from an organization along the way. It is a simple yet effective model that considers the whole journey from a customer's perspective.

The customer journey mapping system shifts an organization's thinking to a place of improving from the customer's perspective. We will focus on this journey for the remainder of this book, analyzing each stage of the journey and exploring best practice techniques to deliver better value and delight for customers.

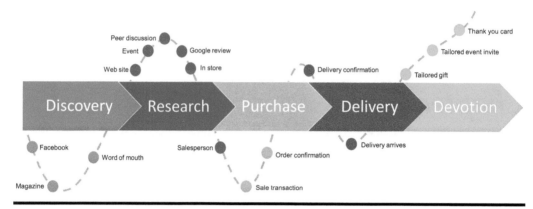

Figure 7.1   The Customer's Journey.

Chapter 8

Discovery

"Discovery" is the initial phase in a customer's buying journey where a customer does not realize that they have a problem to resolve or an opportunity to improve. They are unaware that you and your organization exist and could help them in achieving their goals. All of your existing customers at some stage did not know of you or your organization. Something triggered them to look, and somehow they discovered you. Do you know how they discovered you?

Agile Sales takes a scientific approach to "Discovery." By understanding who your potential customers could be and identifying who they are and what they are doing on a day-to-day basis, you can start to build approaches to help them discover you with value and delight. For the salesperson, "Discovery" requires understanding the customer's world, showing empathy to this, and understanding the ways that you can connect with value and delight. We have covered many techniques already which help build this understanding.

This chapter will concentrate on the following actions that will help you build a proactive approach for helping customer personas discover you:

1. Build your target cohort.
2. Build a foundation of trust with your customer.
3. Connect with abundance.

These actions will help your ideal customer personas discover you and your organization with value and delight. This will start the buying journey with a persona in a way that will ultimately help determine your success.

Step 1: Build Your Target Cohort

A salesperson without a target cohort of customers is unlikely to be focused. They will be running around, fighting fires, and trying to deal with everything that comes across their desk. They are like a ship in a storm without a rudder. I have often heard them being called loose cannons. Focus is crucial in sales excellence endeavors. We have covered the fact that the more we can focus our energy on where we can be most successful, the more success we will have.

We have previously covered how to define a target cohort within Agile Sales Concept 1 – customer understanding. As a refresher, the steps are as follows:

1. Conduct a Pareto analysis of your existing customers, and profile the organizations and decision-making personas you have been most successful with.
2. Use appropriate customer understanding tools to gain insights and build awareness of customers and their world.
3. Build a cohort of target organizations and decision-making personas. Look at the tail of your customer database for companies similar to the ones you are having the most success with. They are typically there, already purchasing from you, just not much as yet.

Once the cohort list of target personas has been developed, they need to be entered into the opportunity Kanban as "suspects." The salesperson then needs to progress each persona through the Kanban (buying journey) at an even flow to avoid overburden or underburden, tracking key leading metrics, continuously improving as they go, overcoming challenges, and innovating.

A cohort chart (Figure 8.1) can be used to create a visual display of the progress of target personas along the buying journey. The chart plots the percentage of target personas at each stage of the buying journey over time. The thicknesses of the different colors represent the percentage of target customers at each step of the sales process at a particular time. Bottlenecks or overburden at stages will show up through large bands of color. Gaps that occur or stages of underburden in the pipeline can be seen as thin or non-existent lines of color.

In this example, 100% of the target list are suspects at the start of the financial year. By the end of quarter one, 50% are still "suspects," 25% are at the "lead" stage, 10% at "understand", 10% at "present," and 5% at "close" and "won." The goal of this chart is to evenly move all deals to 100% "won" if possible, over time. Of course, a 100% win rate is outstanding. You may

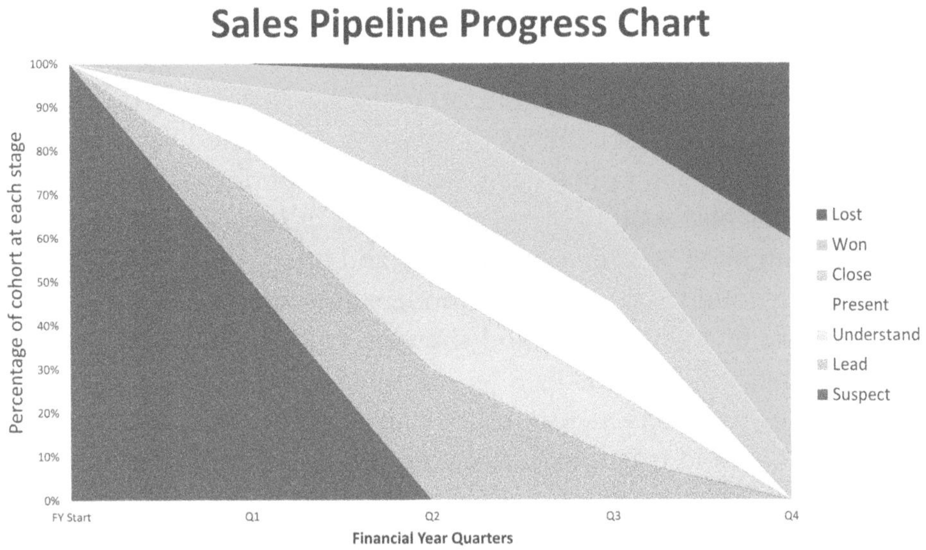

Sales Pipeline Progress Chart

Figure 8.1 Sales Pipeline Cohort Chart.

end up with a percentage of deals that are "won" and "lost," giving you a win–loss ratio.

The cohort target list, coupled with a Kanban system and cohort chart, can be used for account management as well as for business development. An account manager can be given a target cohort of existing customers to focus on throughout a financial year. Key steps and activities to take customers through over the year can be defined and tracked using both the Kanban and cohort chart. This is similar to monitoring opportunities through a sales process.

It is crucial for both business development and account management to have a defined journey to take target accounts through to deliver higher value and delight. The remainder of this book will explore concepts and approaches that you may wish to adopt to develop your team's strategy for customer service.

Step 2: Build a Foundation of Trust with Your Customer

The Importance of Empathy

Empathy is vital in building relatedness with a customer and, through this, developing the foundation for a business partner relationship. Showing empathy requires you to understand a person first.

Showing empathy is impossible without understanding their world, connecting with their experiences, and feeling these yourself.

Many researchers have studied empathy and human connection. I believe there may be no more important work than that completed by Dr. Stephen Covey. Dr. Covey studied human effectiveness and performance, which culminated in his best-selling book *The 7 Habits of Highly Effective People* (Covey). The 5th habit, "Seek first to understand, then to be understood," is essential. Covey found that the skill of understanding someone or something deeply first, listening with intent, and showing empathy provides the foundation for relatedness and trust.

Think of a time you (as a customer) engaged with a salesperson and did not feel that you could trust them. Did you feel like they had an agenda and didn't really care about you or that they just wanted to make a quick sale? How did this make you feel? Have you dealt with this person ongoing?

Several years ago, I was looking to purchase a utility vehicle, commonly called a Ute in Australia. I had always dreamed of owning a particular brand and model. I went into my local dealership and was met by a salesperson. He immediately started to probe me about the car I was looking for and quickly took me to the vehicle in question and started to give me his product pitch.

This salesperson was dealing with me – a person who actually wanted to buy the car already. Yet, he took no time to understand who I was and what my background, goals, and needs were. Instead, he instantly started to pitch the car at me, a car I already knew in detail. The story gets worse. I asked him to send a quote through to my wife as I was heading overseas for a week, which he agreed to do. The next day he called my wife and told her that she needed to come into the car yard to finalize the deal. He said to her that he would provide her a quote during this visit face to face and that he could not quote her otherwise.

My wife felt like she was being manipulated and that he was trying to push her into signing a deal while I was away. This was the worst experience as a customer that I have had in my life. We ended up buying a completely different brand of utility. This salesperson made all of the mistakes from the start. He did not take the time to understand us, showed no empathy, displayed bad manners and language, and did not quote us transparently. He should have been able to quickly close this deal with full margin.

Often it comes back to our perception of the salesperson's intent to help us (the customer) versus help themselves. If the salesperson is genuinely going to help the customer, they need to understand and relate to the customer first. If a customer believes the salesperson is coming from a place of taking the time and doing the research to understand them, a foundation of trust will be formed. This will benefit both parties.

Trust is what creates the foundation of any successful relationship. This approach takes a little more time upfront to research and build but provides returns tenfold later through the sales process, with faster deal closing, higher conversion rate, higher margins, and higher net sales.

Understanding and Relating to Customers

Relatedness follows initial, empathetic research. We are naturally drawn to those we can relate to, the people we share things in common with. The paradigms we have made throughout our life define what we believe in and enjoy. Paradigms are, in basic terms, the pathways in our brains, created through base mental wiring and our experiences in our life. Our history, together with our goals and aspirations, define us, and consequently play a significant role in who we relate to and trust. If you take time to understand an individual's personal background, goals, aspirations, and challenges, you have the foundation for creating a feeling of relatedness and trust.

If you then gain an understanding of the organizational culture where the customer works, you will be able to take the customer–salesperson relationship to an entirely new level. Organizational factors influence us no matter how much we think that they don't. When we join an organization, we are connecting with a group of people who tell similar historical stories and have equal core values, purpose, and goals. We are all influenced by the measures that are placed on us. They show whether we are achieving or not and determine if we receive a bonus. You often find people who share the core values and purpose of an organization stay with that organization for an extended period. They feel comfortable with that organization as their culture and belief aligns with the organization, providing them comfort and the feeling of fitting in.

Gaining an understanding of both personal and organizational background, goals, aspirations, and challenges, with each key decision-making persona, enables the development of long-lasting relationships.

You don't have to wait until you meet someone to start studying them. It is not difficult to research initial information about an organization and key decision-makers' backgrounds and direction in our technological world. When researching online or face to face, remember the three key elements (Figure 8.2) of

Figure 8.2 Key Elements for Understanding Your Customer.

1. Background,
2. Direction, and
3. Challenges moving forward.

Persona Background

LinkedIn makes available background information such as past job roles, connections, references of previous work, and skills. You can find schooling information, groups, and organizations that your potential client follows and common associations that you share. You can also research the client's culture by interpreting how their summary is written and asking questions like "is this client absorbed in self-preservation endeavors or externally focused on helping others?" You can review the recommendations section to read what others write about them and glean from this some initial behavioral insights.

Persona Direction

Again, through LinkedIn, you can find directional information by reading the bio, viewing posts they like and comment on, and the key skills they are learning and being recognized for. Some people write their purpose and even future goals into their bio. Google searches, as well as other social media tools such as Facebook, Twitter, and Instagram, can also be useful in discovering more about the profile and direction of potential clients.

Persona Challenges

Information on a persona's challenges may also be emphasized at times through their LinkedIn bio. You can identify difficulties in the persona's directional goals within the organizational analysis. Physically, you can also put yourself in the persona's shoes. Consider their background and future goals and think about the challenges they would be facing in moving forward.

Organizational Background

Gaining an understanding of the organization is also much simpler today than it was when I started selling before the Internet. There are various places to find organizational information, and this is very similar to understanding the experience of an individual. When researching an organization's background and culture, you are looking for data such as

- Their history,
- When they were founded,
- By who and why,
- Key milestones throughout their history,
- Who their customers are,
- What industries they work in,
- Their competitors and key challenges they have faced in the past competitively,
- Culture – core values and purpose/mission,
- Organizational structure, and
- Key decision-makers.

Typically, organizations publicly promote this information in the "About Us" section of their website and through media releases, which can be found on a company's blog or through an Internet search.

Organizational Direction and Challenges

The "About Us" section on company websites also contains a whole host of information that can reveal organizational direction and challenges. Reading annual reports, if the company is publicly listed, can bring to light strategic prerogatives and critical measures of success that they are focused on. Chairman/CEO/President's letters are also useful. You can gain a deeper understanding of why an organization is focusing on key strategic elements and what has led them to this.

Some of the crucial directional data to look for are

- Vision,
- Objectives,
- Goals,
- Strategies, and
- Strategic Measures.

Media channels do not miss much concerning medium to large organizational action. Media releases and reports highlight recent activity, results, and measures. These will provide you an understanding of current corporate challenges.

Publicly listed organizations have this information readily available online. With private organizations, traditional approaches are often required to conduct profiling.

Traditional Methods of Profiling

If there is limited information on the web for an organization, or a key decision-maker has totally avoided the Internet and social media, you need to fall back on traditional approaches.

Firstly, do you know someone who knows them or their organization? Secondly, what associations and other organizations are they linked with? Thirdly, how can you connect with others in these groups to conduct some initial research on the organization and key decision-makers?

The knowledge you gained through the persona and empathy mapping will help you in planning how you can more traditionally research and connect with a target persona.

Example: Connecting with Customers

CameraPro is a fantastic multi-channel (online, phone, in-store) retailer. Their purpose is to inspire and empower others to create a better world for themselves and the planet through visual mediums and technology (cameras, video recorders, and accessories). They incorporate visuality into everything they do. They have developed a great graphic to help their sales team remember the key elements of customer understanding and research (Figure 8.3).

This image is used in sales training and coaching. It aligns with the company's customer focus of helping customers on their journey from base camp to summit, one camp at a time. The mountain analogy helps the team to understand the base camp position for customers. What has brought their customers to where they are now? What path have they traveled in their life to get to today? What motivated them to begin photography? Where are they now in their journey?

Through this research, a CameraPro team member finds relatedness with the customer. All salespeople are photographers or videographers themselves. This fact is shared at the right time, building further rapport and trust.

The summit analogy helps team members to remember to ask a customer about their goals, purpose, and vision for the future.

Using this knowledge, the salesperson identifies how they can help the customer, about what the next site is to focus on, and what the next camp is to help them reach. They finish the line of questioning by asking the customer what challenges they perceive moving forward. By showing empathy to this and again assisting the customer form ideas, the team member can help them on their journey to their next camp.

Figure 8.3   CameraPro's Visual Customer Journey.

Illustrations like this one help to build a story and visually depict essential processes. This improves memory and, ultimately, performance in the process.

Researching the personal and organizational background and direction and challenges of key decision-makers builds empathy and helps identify relatedness. With this, you can provide your expertise and genuinely help customers to achieve their goals. This enables you to create a foundation for a long-lasting relationship.

Step 3: Connecting with Abundance

This concept is about connecting with targeted decision-makers with value and delight right from the beginning of the customer's buying journey. It promotes starting from a position of abundance and interdependence, rather than desperation and dependence.

Traditionally, many salespeople have pushed themselves on decision-makers, by cold calling and pitching at how amazing their products and services are and why they should meet. This approach builds a perception of desperation in the minds of the targeted customer. It is not a pleasurable experience for the persona, and I don't know of many salespeople who actually enjoy it either. A lot of marketing traditionally pushes offers and bold statements on customers, again coming across as desperation and more of an annoyance than anything else.

Figure 8.4 shows an example of the customer perception of a salesperson. The scale of value and delight a persona perceives rises as you move up each level.

A customer's perception originates from two key factors:

1. The language the salesperson uses, and
2. The push or pull approach – is the salesperson creating the desire for the customer to reach out and connect with them or pushing themselves on the customer?

The lowest level of value possible is that of the vendor. If you are at the vendor level, you are most likely using cold calling methods, demonstrating no initial awareness of yourself or your organization. You will be using product-focused language and using statements like "we make and sell" these products and services. You are pushing yourself onto the customer.

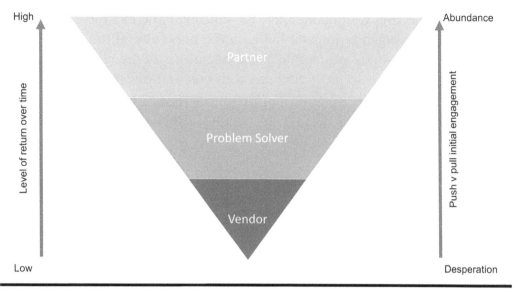

Figure 8.4   Customer Initial Perception.

The next level is the problem solver. This salesperson has done some initial research and demonstrated an understanding of a common problem for the persona. They would have made initial contact with an introduction and provided some basic data on the identified problem. They may then call the persona and discuss the issue and how they may be able to help.

The next level is a partner. This salesperson has comprehensively researched the persona and their organization. They have insights about the personal and organizational background, direction, and challenges. They have identified unique opportunities to connect with this persona, through an industry event or through a mutual colleague. They have found a high level of relatedness with the persona as well as with fellow associates.

Salespeople operating at the level of partner tailor their approach to the individual they are looking to connect with. They show empathy in their communication, demonstrate relatedness, and expertly identify value-adding ways to help a target customer discover them. A pull approach to connecting with relatedness and value is created with this approach. The customer reaches out with motivation and desire to connect, based on their perception of the salesperson as a partner.

When we connect with desperation and dependence (such as in cold calling), the customer perceives us as a vendor. This translates into a low value, low power relationship, delivering low levels of return over time for the seller. Your margins for the initial sale are squeezed, and it is typically hard to retain the customer for any length of time.

When connecting with abundance, the customer anchors their perception of you and your organization at a higher level, hopefully, at the level of a partner. High-value perception at the beginning of the relationship encourages customers to move forward with you and pay the asking price for a product and service. They will likely develop loyalty, providing, of course, that they continue to receive value and delight. This delivers a high level of return over time for the sales organization.

Connecting with abundance firstly requires an understanding of your customer by conducting a thorough analysis of ideal customers and personas previously mentioned (persona and empathy maps). By doing this analysis, you will gain insights into where, when, and how you could engage key personas with abundance and start the buying journey with them from a position of a partner. You are looking for ways and critical times to help the persona discover you, and this prompts them to engage you. I call this abundant pull-based "Discovery" rather than the traditional desperate push-based "Discovery," such as cold calling and product and price marketing.

You will be able to identify the best medium/forum to use to connect with abundance for a persona, be it through internet sites, events, radio, podcasts, television, magazines, or related organizations. You will be able to identify the best time to connect with them: time of the year, month, week, and day. You will be able to develop ideas on how to best connect with a persona to deliver value and delight right away.

I have facilitated this type of customer analysis with many companies and will give two examples here.

Example: CameraPro Customer Analysis

CameraPro discovered new information about "Margaret," one of their key personas. "Margaret" is an older retiree who travels extensively after retiring and is looking for a new hobby, to build social connections, and to learn new skills.

Traditionally, CameraPro would connect with "Margaret" after her initial travel when she is settled back home and ready to discover a new hobby (entering photography). After their analysis, CameraPro now looks to help "Margaret" discover them during her holiday planning right after retiring. CameraPro team members now attend travel expos and travel forums and have formed partnerships and special offers with travel agencies. It is a brilliant "Discovery" approach as a person often thinks about which camera that they will take on holiday. "Margaret" can enjoy a holiday with a good camera and expand her creativity, set new goals, and develop new skills with photography at the same time.

Example: The Winson Group Customer Analysis

The Winson Group discovered that several of their key personas work within the manufacturing industry and rely heavily upon feedback from peers when looking for ways to improve and overcome challenges. As a result of this, sales executives from the Winson Group now attend industry peer networking events relevant to these personas. During these events, team members connect one-on-one with the key personas and begin immediately to help them with the improvement goals and challenges they are facing. This approach also brought another benefit to the Winson Group. As they are a manufacturer also, they were able to establish and host their own value-added industry networking events. This allowed key personas to visit their manufacturing sites for tours and see firsthand activities focused on best practices. This is one of the best examples of pull-based "Discovery," as you are pulling key decision-makers into your business as part of these industry learning events.

These types of abundant "Discovery" approaches are utilized by organizations all around the world. Every day we are directly and subliminally influenced by organizations helping us discover them with abundance without even knowing it.

Relatedness When Connecting

There is an old saying, "Birds of a feather flock together," that expresses the human need for relatedness: our desire to be part of a group with similar traits and characteristics.

Neuroscientists in recent times have discovered mirror neurons in the human brain. These are the specific cells responsible for sensing emotions and feelings in others to seek relatedness, showing empathy, and building connections (Rifkin, 2010). This leads to the belief that our brains are hardwired to build a connection with others who show us empathy and who have common traits and characteristics that we can relate to. This is a natural behavior for most of us when we meet someone for the first time. We ask questions about the other person and share common insights about ourselves when we find areas of relatedness. As these commonalities are shared, people experience a positive emotion, the energy in the conversation lifts, and both parties smile and are pleased with the connection found. Humans are designed to relate to others, and even the introverted, quiet individual still desires relatedness.

How often do you share relatedness-based information that you have discovered when connecting initially with a customer?

Some examples of shared aspects that may be found are

Personal commonalities with decision-makers/personas

1. High school or university attended,
2. Region where you live,
3. Age,
4. Sport/sporting team followed,
5. Hobbies,
6. Study areas,
7. Marital status,
8. Life stages,
9. Friends in common,
10. Beliefs,
11. Challenges, and
12. Future goals.

Organization commonalities

1. Type of company, i.e. private/family-owned, publicly listed,
2. Locations around a country or globally,
3. Values and behaviors,
4. Company age,
5. Historical commonalities,
6. Competitors,
7. Vision for the future,
8. Purpose/mission,
9. Strategic focus areas, and
10. Measures of strategic focus.

Discovering these areas of relatedness can help you gain insight into the unique ways that you can connect with abundance, value, and delight and anchor your relationship at a high level.

Example: CameraPro's Key Persona

A great example of this approach comes, again, from CameraPro. They identified and created a key persona of an engineer named "Brett" as part of their Pareto analysis and persona creation. "Brett" is into technology and photography; he seeks in-depth and accurate knowledge of the latest technology. "Brett" is introverted and analytical and is motivated by the new challenges of technology. Understanding this, the CameraPro team came up with the concept of hosting technological days in store. They invite camera product brand owners into the store as well as the "Brett's" of their world to gain insights into the latest and greatest technology. They set up photography scenarios at these events where "Brett" can test the new technology practically. They promote these events through web and print media relevant to technical engineering types like "Brett."

Multiple Touchpoints

Connecting with personas is not necessarily a one-off occasion that will lead naturally into a buying journey/opportunity. It is essential not to fall into the trap of ignoring any personas/decision-makers who do not respond to your first communication attempt. Many studies have investigated how many connections or touchpoints are required before trust is built, leading to an opportunity. Researchers say 4 touchpoints, some 6, some 15. I believe that the level of value and delight provided at each touchpoint will determine how long it takes you to build trust. The higher the value and delight, the fewer touchpoints will be required to build trust and enter a value-added sales cycle for both parties (Figure 8.5).

Multiple touchpoints allow an organization to tailor lead generation campaigns in a series of value-added touchpoints over a period. These moments can build upon each other, creating a value-added brand for yourself and your organization. This approach requires sales and marketing to work closely together, which the multi-level Agile RVM approach will help foster.

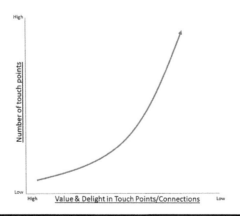

Figure 8.5   Touchpoint Comparison.

I will discuss two examples of multiple touchpoints – one from Signet and the other from Six Degrees Executive.

Example: Signet, Multiple Touchpoints

A compelling case that I am currently observing is the targeted multiple touchpoint approach being implemented by Signet, focused on the persona of "Barry." "Barry" is a warehouse leader. He is a man's man, dealing with a lot of stress day to day in his work, which is largely time based with many safety and people challenges. "Barry" lives in the suburbs and enjoys football, cricket, and fishing. He values catching up with peers and mates for the support it provides as well as having a laugh to break the stress of his day job. "Barry" uses social media and will communicate with friends via social media.

Signet developed an initial campaign via social media that provides "Barry" a good laugh during his day. He can share this easily with his peers and mates. This first touchpoint is a series of short videos featuring "Canmaster Smash," a brilliant Australian street entertainer who produces the most fantastic beats and music using industrial items. Signet have sponsored "Canmaster" to use their own industrial products in his performances. They have filmed several short videos that are highly entertaining and can't help but put a smile on your dial! Singular videos of "Canmaster" are published each month, providing ongoing enjoyment and the initial three or so touchpoints that build brand recognition and, more importantly, trust.

A second campaign offers "Barry" a variety of short snips of a documentary-style video of Australia's "Jinja Assassin." The "Jinja Assassin" is a highly entertaining, competitive air guitarist and is sponsored by Signet. He rocks his socks off in the competitions he enters and provides a good laugh and high-energy fun. These fourth and fifth touchpoints offer some light relief for "Barry," and again can be shared easily with his peers and mates.

The sixth and seventh touchpoints are direct, relevant case studies and articles to help "Barry" in his workplace. These will include insights and unique approaches that Signet can provide that can help "Barry" improve safety, quality, and productivity.

Different "Barry's" will connect with Signet at various times throughout this multiple touchpoint approach to a buying journey. Particular "Barry's" who Signet would really like to connect with may have a salesperson make a direct approach with a high-value focus.

Example: Six Degrees Executive, Multiple Touchpoints

Six Degrees Executive is a leading, specialist executive recruitment consultancy firm. They recruit executives for many industrial: marketing, digital, retail, sales, supply chain, procurement, and operations.

They have developed a targeted approach for several key senior executive decision-making personas who they engage with. This insight has been provided by one of their consultants, Dan Pirrone. Six Degrees Executive have found that to sell an idea, particularly in highly commoditized sectors, the key is to position yourself and your business as subject matter experts. You have valuable knowledge that your client won't be able to find anywhere else. To drive conversation away from price, toward value, you need to be able to demonstrate a higher level of sophistication than your competition. A great way to encourage this passively is to facilitate local events, free of any pitch, that simply aim to share cutting edge ideas or thought leadership. These events will work by driving client engagement proactively, shifting your sales process from less of a push to more of a pull.

Six Degrees Executive see this as an essential pillar of their business development strategy. They must remain at the forefront of their respective sectors to stay engaged with the most dynamic and high-achieving professionals in the market. To ensure they maintain a healthy pipeline to service their clients, their "Thought Leadership Event Series" acts as a lightning rod for their specialist sectors.

Events such as these can and should vary. They could be industry/discipline networking events with a keynote speaker, industry roundtables or forums, or panel-style Q&A. It is imperative to choose a venue that will enhance the function. For example, an event or function space would suit networking events and panel-style Q&A. Forums can be hosted onsite to allow for more of firsthand experience.

In facilitating an event, you need to recognize the significant challenges in your sector and then demonstrate insight and practices that haven't been seen before. By understanding the voice of your customer, you should already have an idea of these challenges (as they should already comprise part of your solution). The ideal is to have someone deliver this on your behalf. You want to create an environment that fosters ideas, not pitching or pushing. People are far more likely to attend an industry roundtable or Q&A event with significant leaders than to sit down and have you pitch to them about a product, no matter what the environment is.

To foster a successful event, a level of networking is required, as the focus needs to be on the credibility of the speakers. Often though, you can reach out to a client business (particularly one of your closest partners) to help you facilitate this. Outside of that, asking not-for-profit organizations and educational institutions for facilitative help can be a benefit, particularly if there is an element of sponsorship or fundraising for a philanthropic cause.

Once you have determined your topic, your speaker/s, and style of forum (Q&A, seminar, panel discussion), the next step is to form up your invite list. To really drive sales in your event, you need to keep the guest list manageable, not only from a venue perspective, but also in organizing invites and then, most importantly, at the end of the function, where you leverage from the event to generate business. If in doubt, remember the classic saying, "less is more." You want to target people who will be affected by the topic and who will have the appetite to purchase your product. It is imperative to ensure you have targeted the key decision-makers in your invite list.

In reaching out initially, the conversation should be light. The reason for calling is to inform the client of the event and why you feel it may be of interest to them. Remember to finish your research on their business and be able to articulate this concisely to engage them. Give a brief overview of the topic, the format and speakers, and some insight you have of their business/industry as to why it would be of interest (again, demonstrating credibility). This will often be one of the most straightforward cold calls you will make. You aren't selling anything, you simply felt they would benefit from attending and wanted to do them a favor by informing them.

The next step from here is to arrange the invitations, which can be automated via your Customer Relationship Management (CRM) program. (A CRM program is a customer management software used by organizations to manage customer data and interactions.) Ensure the data collated allows you to facilitate follow-up after the event, including business, role, and contact information. Include specifics around the topic, speakers, and why it would be of interest/relevance. You want to ensure that these key decision-makers are in the room and don't palm it off to a subordinate to take notes for them.

As a rule of thumb, despite RSVPs, you will have between 15% and 40% drop-off for the event. Ensure you follow up with clients who haven't officially lodged an RSVP, and then send a reminder a few days later. There will always be people who have to drop out at the last minute due to work emergencies, family requirements, traffic, etc. Ensure that your guest list is a little inflated to cover this drop-off.

If you manage to achieve 100% attendance from a guest list, then be sure to reach out to me. I would be very interested in writing my next book around how you achieved this!

At the event itself, as host, you should know everyone in the room. Ensure you are working to make introductions with clients who may benefit from meeting new contacts. Again, this is all about you, displaying your knowledge in the space, and providing value and insight. Ensure that you address the group from beginning to end and are introducing the event and speakers, including a brief background. Ensure you have prepared some questions or topics for discussion should the audience be a little slow to engage. This is especially relevant if you are hosting a breakfast event!

Event follow-up is responsible for driving ROI (return of investment) from this event. Ensure you have contacted every attendee within the week via phone – again, this is an easy conversation to make, as you frame it purely around their feedback from the event. Probe around what they found to be the biggest takeaway for them, as this will give you more insight around their business priorities.

It also helps to have some collateral available, like links to articles or reports that they may find valuable. At the end of this call, set a meeting to discuss their challenges further. You should have a good idea at this point as to where you can provide value to your client, as they have just told you! Be able to articulate an example of a similar initiative you have led for another client. Again – do not sell here! This is simply a chance to sit down and get more of an idea of their main problems and why they are unique so that you can work out how you can tailor a solution to help them.

For those candidates who couldn't attend, it is worth reaching out to give them an overview of the discussion and main ideas from others in similar roles/businesses. Again, you can then drive the conversation around more of a "Discovery" and lead into where you will be able to assist. It would also be worth composing a follow-up email to be mass mailed to attendees and those who were unable to make it. Overview in this email core topics, and include some talking head quotes from other attendees as to their biggest learnings (with their permission of course). Conclude with links to any collateral that may be of interest. This also gives you the option, if any contacts declined to attend the event, to touch base again in a week. You can ask if they had reviewed the collateral and, yet again, try to secure a meeting.

The entire process for this event will probably take four to eight weeks, as you want to give your contacts plenty of notice to ensure they are available to attend. At this point, however, you will have had between three to six points of contact with the client (intro call, invite email, confirmation call/email, a quick chat on the day, follow-up call, insight collateral email, client meeting).

This multiple touchpoint approach provides a great example of a different "Discovery" strategy that may help you and your organization.

Please remember to consider the customer perception of the salespeople model (Figure 8.4) while planning your approach.

I believe there is still a place for a direct call but only after other value-added connections through a multiple touchpoint approach have been made. This is because our initial emotional reaction to being engaged by someone we don't know is a threat response. Observe your feelings the next time you are approached by someone you have not met or spoken to before. Unless you are a social butterfly, do you feel a sense of awkwardness or unease? This is your brain triggering a threat response to this stranger you have not as yet met. I guess that this natural response has evolved over history within humans. A few hundred years ago, it would have been wise to perceive a newcomer as a potential threat.

Many studies have discovered how many times we need to be engaged by someone before we drop the threat response and start to trust. The results of these studies vary between four and eight times. The exact number does not matter. Remember that the multiple touchpoint approach pinpoints personas, reduces their threat response, and ensures they feel more comfortable with you and your organization. This will help with the success of your direct call should you need to make one.

If you do need to make a direct call, following a multiple touchpoint approach, I recommend utilizing the "Hard to Get Meeting Process" that we will explore next. The process has been developed considering executives' busy schedules and, typically, rapid annoyance responses to the multiple messages left by salespeople asking for a return call.

The "Hard to Get Meeting Process"

For some reason, we make prospect calls in a totally different way to the way we would call to make an appointment in our everyday life. We put on a cheesy voice, hype it up, and make bold statements to try and entice the persona we are targeting to meet with us. I have found that being natural, honest, and to the point works much better.

The "Hard to Get Meeting Process" (Figure 8.6) is built on this belief and works best if you use a normal voice, don't hype it up, and don't make a pitch. This may be asking you to undo years of habit, but I know it will save you and your target persona a lot of time and bother. The process is the same one that you would use if you were busy and wanting to set a meeting promptly with a friend, family member, or supplier.

Call & state why, where and when you want to meet (Typically you will get a voice mail, leave this statement on the message)

 Send a proposed **meeting planner**, restating why you want to meet and prompting them to cancel or propose another time if needed.

 Call on the morning of the meeting if you don't get a response, if you get their voice mail state please call if any issues with meeting, otherwise you look forward to meeting them later today.

 Go to the **meeting**, if they stand you up it is their bad and they will try and make it up to you.

Figure 8.6 Hard to Get Meeting Process.

Example: The "Hard to Get Meeting Process"

I have heard Dan Pirrone, from Six Degrees Executive (who kindly wrote the section on their multiple touchpoint approach), use this technique many times. Dan is extremely good at the process as he is naturally genuine and to the point when engaging customers. Dan works from a targeted cohort; he knows the organizations and key personas within them that he focuses on. You know from the case study he provided on Six Degrees Executive multiple touchpoint approach that he is not initially cold calling. The initial call would only occur after a persona has been through their multiple touchpoint approach.

Dan sorts his target cohort list by postcode and plans his days around regions. This keeps meetings close together and saves the waste of drive time, enabling him to get through more meetings in the day. A few months ahead, Dan will start his value-added multiple touchpoint approach for the new persona he is targeting. Three to four weeks ahead of the planned meeting date is a perfect time to call. This timing ensures that a proposed meeting is not too far out or too close. (A salesperson who does not plan three to four weeks ahead is doing themselves a disservice. Senior decision makers' calendars are always completely booked one to two weeks ahead. Attempting to set a meeting three to four weeks out gives you much higher chance of successfully setting a meeting.) Dan will call the personas who have not already connected through the previous multi-touch point warm-up process.

Typically when calling, Dan gets their voice mail. He states his name, company, role, and why he is calling and suggests a day and time for the meeting when he is in their area. Dan completes the call mentioning that he will send through a projected meeting planner for this time and that they can cancel or suggest another more appropriate time if need be. Proposing another time is strategically placed at the completion of the call, as it puts this option front of mind (rather than canceling).

Dan then sends through the projected calendar entry. This is created from a Microsoft template, saving writing time as he can simply modify the template as required. A few options typically play out for Dan. Option one: the persona accepts the meeting. Option two: they decline and give a reason which Dan then uses to hedge and propose another time. Option three: there is no response.

In the morning, on the days of the meetings, if a response has not been received, Dan will call the contact. Again, he typically gets their voice mail. He simply states on the message that he has the meeting in the calendar and they can call if there are any issues. Otherwise, he looks forward to meeting them later that day. If someone does not want to meet, Dan finds he receives an apologetic call and then simply proposes another time that suits both parties.

I personally find this process, running in conjunction with the warm-up multiple touchpoint campaigns, delivers a 90% hit rate for setting initial meetings with target personas. If you do not get these results, analyze the "Why You Want to Meet" statement that you use in the initial phone call and meeting planner.

Developing Your "Why You Want to Meet" Statement

The following two aspects help you to succeed with your "why" statement:

1. Link it to a strategic focus area you have discovered through your research on them or their company.
2. Keep it humble, prompt, and straightforward.

During my times in sales, I have found that the more straightforward your "why" statement is, the better. I typically state the strategic focus area of theirs that I had seen. I mentioned that I was their account manager and that I may be able to help them with their strategic focus area. I would not be trying to meet if I did not think there was a way that I could be of service. I would then mention that it would be great to put a face to a name for the future.

I have helped so many salespeople improve their success rate with outbound calling, by purely shifting them to the "put a face to each other for the future" statement. I typically find salespeople who have an inferior hit rate are talking and pitching too much in the initial call rather than keeping it simple and to the point.

Once you have the initial meeting with a customer, you are entering the "Research" phase of their buying journey. This is where the rubber hits the road concerning the sales cycle. Many techniques are useful in leading a client through this phase of the customer buying journey with value and delight.

Suggested Actions for "Discovery"

"Discovery" is such an essential part of the buying and sales journey. A practical approach to helping personas discover you and your organization will help keep your opportunity pipeline full. "Discovery" requires good collaboration between marketing and sales to be truly successful.

Some suggested actions are as follows:

1. Conduct a Pareto analysis of your existing customers, and profile the organizations and decision-making personas you have been most successful with.
2. Build a cohort of target organizations and decision-making personas. Look at the tail of your customer database for companies similar to the ones you are having the most success with. They are typically there, already purchasing from you, just not much as yet.
3. "Research" the target organizations and personas to understand their background, direction, and challenges.
4. Develop a multiple touchpoint warm-up process in collaboration with marketing or other support teams if possible.
5. Practice the "Hard to Get Meeting Process" and your "Why You Want to Meet" statement.
6. Make the process visual using a Kanban system. Focus on keeping the pipeline even and full.

These steps will provide you with a quality flow of leads to begin moving through the rest of the buying journey with value and delight. You will be starting the buying journey from the position of a partner rather than a vendor. This will ultimately help your success rate and margins over time.

Chapter 9

Research

Customers enter the "Research" phase on a buying journey when they are motivated to answer outstanding questions, looking to be reassured emotionally before moving forward with a purchase. If their questions and concerns are inadequately answered, and they are not provided enough motivation to change, people generally forget about the purchase as it declines in priority.

For a salesperson, the "Research" phase is about helping to answer questions and concerns promptly for customers in a way that helps build motivation for them to move forward with the buying journey.

What Answers Are Customers Looking For?

What are customers typically looking for from salespeople? I have conducted many deep-dive customer surveys with sales organizations, and each time, two common themes arise:

1. Help us solve problems that are impacting us achieving our goals.
2. Help us improve in your areas of expertise to achieve our objectives.

Customers in today's market are looking for salespeople to elevate their focus and act more like abundant consultants rather than product salespersons. They seek more of a partner relationship. Their ideal salesperson works in their best interest, helps to overcome obstacles, and makes improvements to help them achieve their goals, year after year.

Although this research highlights that customers are seeking higher value from salespeople, many other surveys show otherwise. Some show that up to 70% of customers believe they do not receive any value from a salesperson. Why does this disconnect occur? One review shows that customers are looking for value from salespeople; another shows they believe they do not receive value from salespeople.

The disconnect is primarily due to the traditional push-based sales approach to engaging customers. Traditionally in sales, we have been taught how to sell products and services, find the need/pain, and pitch the features and benefits of the product to win the business. The problem with this approach is that customers are not looking for you to pitch a product at them. They want salespeople who will use their knowledge, products, and services to solve problems and help them improve.

It is a subtle adjustment required, but one that will enable salespeople to regain control and deliver higher value and delight to their customers. The salesperson's ability to deeply "Research" during the customer's buying journey will significantly affect the "Purchase" phase that follows.

Asking the Right Questions, the Right Way

Many sales authors have written about the 80/20 rule (Pareto Principle). This states that during the "Research" phase of the customer's buying journey, the salesperson should use open probes to keep the customer talking 80% of the time and only speak 20% of the time. I believe this ratio should be tailored to the persona you are meeting with. Some more introverted personas may not want to talk as much as a more extroverted persona. They may find an extended period of open questions and having to talk irritating and stressful.

I have found that most salespeople are skilled at using open probe questioning. The area that salespeople seem to struggle with is elevating these open questions in a consultative way. Salespeople are often measured and rewarded for product sales. So, what typically happens is that salespeople drive a conversation with a customer to find problems and pain, enabling them to pitch products. It is a known behavior resulting from the pressure we are under to make money. The issue is that customers are looking for a salesperson to listen, truly understand themselves and their business, and then find ways they can help.

Asking quality questions, at the right time, allows a salesperson to truly understand a buying persona and their business and is a skill that can be developed and improved over time.

I believe the following areas of focus can really help a salesperson improve their questioning ability:

1. Plan your questions, including the use of profiling data.
2. Elevate your questions.
3. Listen with empathy.
4. Deep dive into key topics.

Question Planning

The purpose of planning your questions is to

■ Reflect on the information you already have about the persona and their organization,
■ Develop questions to gain a deeper understanding, and
■ Demonstrate to the customer that you have done your homework, are prepared, and truly focused on understanding and helping them and their organization.

Planning your questions involves taking the time to think about a meeting you have coming up with a decision-maker. Think about everything you have discovered and researched about this person and their organization through the profiling you have already completed. Use this profiling information to tailor your questions to suit the customer and help structure a quality meeting. I have seen question planning take many forms and don't believe in terming any one way as the "right way." Establishing the approach that suits you and your team should be the focus.

Question Planning Tools

This formal pre-meeting question planning template (Figure 9.1) has a pre-set list of questions that the team has created. It is a system I was introduced to by Gavin Wood, a sales leader who is focused on helping his team achieve their best. Before a meeting, sales team members review the profiling data collected and choose the appropriate items for the upcoming meeting. The template then becomes a guide that they also use to take notes

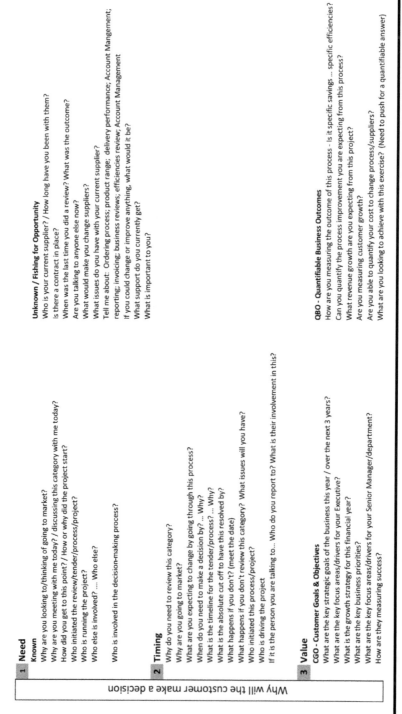

Why will the customer make a decision

1 Need

Known

Why are you looking to/thinking of going to market?
Why are you meeting with me today? / discussing this category with me today?
How did you get to this point? / How or why did the project start?
Who initiated the review/tender/process/project?
Who is running the project?
Who else is involved? …. Who else?

Who is involved in the decision-making process?

Unknown / Fishing for Opportunity

Who is your current supplier? / How long have you been with them?
Is there a contract in place?
When was the last time you did a review? What was the outcome?
Are you talking to anyone else now?
What would make you change suppliers?
What issues do you have with your current supplier?
Tell me about: Ordering process; product range; delivery performance; Account Mangement; reporting; invoicing; business reviews; efficiencies review; Account Management
If you could change or improve anything, what would it be?
What support do you currently get?
What is important to you?

2 Timing

Why do you need to review this category?
Why are you going to market?
What are you expecting to change by going through this process?
When do you need to make a decision by? … Why?
What is the timeline for the tender/process? … Why?
What is the absolute cut off to have this resolved by?
What happens if you don't? (meet the date)
What happens if you don't review this category? What issues will you have?
Who initiated this process/project?
Who is driving the project
If it is the person you are talking to… Who do you report to? What is their involvement in this?

3 Value

CGO - Customer Goals & Objectives

What are the key strategic goals of the business this year / over the next 3 years?
What are the key focus areas/drivers for your Executive?
What is the growth strategy for this financial year?
What are the key business priorities?
What are the key focus areas/drivers for your Senior Manager/department?
How are they measuring success?

QBO - Quantifiable Business Outcomes

How are you measuring the outcome of this process - Is it specific savings … specific efficiencies?
Can you quantify the process improvement you are expecting from this process?
What revenue growth are you expecting from this project?
Are you measuring customer growth?
Are you able to quantify your cost to change process/suppliers?
What are you looking to achieve with this exercise? (Need to push for a quantifiable answer)

Figure 9.1   Formal Pre-Meeting Question Planning Template.

from the responses to each question. This is a highly structured approach which will suit some sales teams and individuals.

The benefit of this approach is that the team shares ideas and captures best practices for use into the future. The downside with this approach is the rigidity it can bring to a meeting with a customer when used poorly. This may lead to a very clinical meeting following a set pattern of questions with the salesperson madly trying to take notes in the right section of the form. Customer service, using empathy and building rapport may be lost.

This simple approach to question planning (Figure 9.2) provides salespeople with insights into great questioning techniques and encourages them to explore their own ideas and strategies for questioning. The questioning planning is structured around the broad topics of persona and organization background, culture, and strategic direction. Team members are trained to review profiling data they had gained on the persona and organization and use this to bullet point some areas to explore further during the meeting. Salespeople during meeting planning "bullet-point" these notes at the top of a page and use this as a checklist to refer to during the meeting. Team members skim over the bullet points at various times during the meeting; they check to see if any topics have not yet been covered.

The benefit of this approach is the fluidity and flow it brings to a meeting. Salespeople do not stick to a rigid list of questions; they merely refer to a bullet list at odd times as a prompt for further discussion. It allows the salesperson to keep their focus on the person they are meeting with, show empathy, and take notes as and when needed to capture key points discussed. The downside of this approach is that it is not so detailed and defined; some salespeople do not gain the benefit of having detailed,

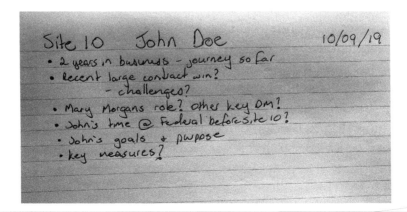

Figure 9.2　Simple Bullet-Point-Checklist Approach.

high-quality questions with them as a prompt. The other negative is that it does not capture and archive great questions for future use.

Tailoring your approach to what best helps the individual salesperson is recommended. In some cases, it may be a blend of the two examples: a cheat sheet of possible questions to refer to before meetings and the more fluid bullet-point prompt approach to refer to during the meeting. Some salespeople may work better with more structure and prefer the full list of pre-defined questions. Others will work best with more coaching and support around improving questioning, coupled with the simple bullet-point-checklist approach. We are all different, and the more we can tailor development to the individual, the greater success we will have.

Elevate Your Conversations

The purpose of elevating your conversation is to gain higher-quality information than your competition and anchor a value-added perception with decision-makers. You are building an impression that you are a consultant who can genuinely help them rather than a salesperson who can sell them a product or service.

To elevate conversations, the level of the questions you ask needs to be raised. Questions should be around the key topics of background, direction, and challenges rather than process, product, and price. The two areas of focus for elevated questions are the decision-maker and then the organization they work for. You may ask yourself, "Should I start with elevated questions relating to the person I am meeting with or their organization?" I believe that how well you already know the customer is how you will decide.

If you are meeting with someone for the first time, there is no pre-existing trusting relationship to launch from. It is more appropriate to begin the conversation around the persona and then move to the organization. Questions focused on the persona will allow you to show empathy, find and demonstrate relatedness, and start forming a level of relationship and trust. Considering this approach, it is always best if you can meet one-on-one with decision-makers during the "Research" phase of their buying journey. This is because it makes it easier to focus on them and ask open questions to truly understand them. It also provides for a safer environment for the person you are meeting with. This can lead to a further uncovering of information about them and their organization that you may not gain if other colleagues were present in the meeting.

Alternatively, if you are meeting with someone you know well, you could start more casually with "How is business going?" "How is the market?" When you have a high level of trust with senior decision-makers, you can open conversation early on these topics that are front of mind for them. This demonstrates that you understand their world and what is most important to them. You are keen to stay up to date so that you can keep helping them wherever you can.

Another element to consider with organizational probing is to include questions on product purpose. Questions around product purpose elevate the product conversation higher than probing for challenges in the areas of the products and services you sell. Product purpose focuses on understanding why a customer uses the products and services you sell in the first place and what purpose or outcome these products and services serve for them.

Consider a photographer who is researching a new camera. They want to purchase a new camera, but why are they buying a camera? What purpose does it serve for them? A photographer might be passionate about wildlife conservation. Perhaps they want to use their photographs to raise awareness of the detriment of endangered wildlife. If you can understand the higher purpose that someone uses the product and service you provide, you are in a position to communicate and help them at an elevated level.

Think about the product purpose for a warehouse manager researching new options in pallet wrap for use within their workplace. Pallets of products are not wrapped in plastic just for the sake of it. The purpose of the product and process is to secure the load throughout the supply chain to ensure the product arrives at its destination in good condition. A quality wrapped pallet also provides for safety throughout the supply chain, eliminating the chance of pallets toppling and injuring people or shifting in transit and causing an accident.

Discussing product purpose is about elevating the conversation to the real reason a product or service is purchased and used by a customer. Questions in this area raise the conversation to a higher level. Insights often result, which the salesperson may not have gained had they kept the conversation focused on the product itself. It is important to note that customers can forget the exact purpose of the product and service you provide and start focusing on base elements such as price. This is a massive risk for customers.

If customers and salespeople lose focus on the true purpose of a product or service, they might purchase/sell an inferior product, costing less upfront but costing a lot more further down the track. This scenario happens every day with both small and large impacts.

Example: Inferior Product "Purchase"

I was once involved with a company that will remain nameless, running a label tender. They were aggressively seeking the best price, and unfortunately, the company I was working for was caught in the vendor trap with everyone else. We lost the business based on price, which the team took hard as they had put a lot of work into the bid.

   Some months later we found out that the labels chosen by the prospective customer were falling off the products they were meant to adhere to. The labels were also damaging the printers they were being run through. The result was a product recall for the company. The company reran the tender process. We approached this tender, determined not to get caught in the vendor trap. We stayed focused on promoting the purpose of the product and the job it needed to do. We ultimately won the second tender, which was brilliant and retained the customer for many years to come.

Our job as abundant salespeople is to help customers sustain focus on what is truly important to them, the people around them, their society, and the planet. We use our knowledge and questioning skills to keep the real purpose of a product, service, or process front of mind. We ultimately help customers make the right decisions for the long term.

Elevated Questions for Personal and Organizational Probing

Personal Background
1. How long have you been with the organization?
2. What roles have you had within the organization?
3. Where have you worked previously?
4. What are the critical functions of your current role?
5. How many employees are there in your team?
6. How do you handle the commute to work?
7. What cultural elements have you developed or are looking to develop in your team?
8. Can you explain more about the XX culture element? We are also looking to develop this in our organization.
9. How do you like to lead improvement or change in your team?
10. How long have you lived in XX?
11. Have you lived overseas?
12. What countries have you lived in?
13. How did you find living in that country?

Personal Direction

1. What is your vision for your team over the next five years?
2. What motivates and drives you and your team?
3. What are your key focus areas, considering your vision for the next few years?
4. What are the key measures you and your team are focused on?
5. What are the challenges you feel that you and your team are going to face?
6. How does this support your goals over the next few years?

Organizational Background

1. How long has the company been in operation?
2. How has the organization evolved to what it is today?
3. What products and services do you distribute?
4. What is the size of the organization? Where are the locations within the region?
5. Who founded the organization?
6. What industries do you operate in?
7. Who are some of your customers?
8. Who do you compete with?
9. What culture is the organization looking to foster?
10. What challenges are you facing with this?
11. How is the organization structured? Who leads each area?
12. With change and improvement, who are the key stakeholders who need to be consulted?

Organizational Direction

1. What is the vision for the organization?
2. Who is leading that vision?
3. How quickly do they want to get there? How are they going about leading the vision?
4. What is the purpose/mission of the company? What does this mean to the CEO?
5. What is the long-term objective of the organization? What is the short-term aim?
6. What are your unique points of difference? What aspects of difference are you looking at to build?
7. What are the key strategies the organization is focused on?
8. What are the key measures the organization is focused on improving?

9. What are the challenges the organization is currently facing on this journey?
10. What challenges do you predict the organization will face in the future on this journey?

Organizational Product Purpose

1. What outcome would you like to achieve with the products we provide?
2. Why is this important to your business, your customers, society, and the planet?
3. What could happen if you don't use the products/services we provide?
4. What challenges are you facing around the outcomes you are aiming to achieve?
5. What would the perfect world look like for you in this area if you had the choice?

If you have not asked questions like these or been involved in executive-level planning and discussions previously, you may feel uncomfortable elevating your conversations. This is no reason to give up! I recommend asking yourself, "What could I do to become comfortable asking these questions?"

You need to practice: try with loved ones first, and fake it until you make it. Sometimes jumping in the deep end and forcing yourself to swim is the only way. A coach or mentor can also help improve your conversational ability; do you have one within your organization? If not, call for support from outside your organization.

Some organizations cascade strategy well to all levels of the organization, including sales teams (Hoshin Kanri). This naturally involves salespeople in historical, cultural, and strategic conversations, developing a better understanding of the process and why these elements are so crucial to senior decision-makers and their organization.

You may think, "I am not talking to high-enough decision-makers. The customers I am talking to would not know or even care about these topics." Do the personas you are currently meeting with have the authority to say, "Yes, I can purchase your product/service," or only say, "No, I don't have the authority to make a purchase," or "I have to take that to my boss to make a decision."

If you are dealing with people who have no authority to purchase, or who could be overruled by someone above them, you need to elevate the decision-maker you are dealing with. Salespeople need to deal with high-level decision-makers, the people who have the authority to say "Yes!"

to purchasing from us. They don't sit back and hope that the lower-level decision-maker they are working with chooses them and then convinces others further up the ladder of this decision. High-performance sales is about leading the sales process with the main stakeholders in the deal directly.

Typically, when you are focused on selling significant deals, the level of decision-maker you need to deal with elevates. The level of questions required to speak their language and elevate yourself to a consultative approach also raises.

Example – Elevating Conversations

One of the best examples I have seen of a sales professional who can talk at elevated levels with senior decision-makers is Chris Jones. It wasn't always this way. When I first met Chris, he was fresh out of university with no background in sales, a young 21-year-old. Chris, like all young salespeople, struggled with confidence when dealing with senior decision-makers. He also fell into the trap of quickly moving a conversation with a customer toward the product he was selling. This was resulting in customers perceiving Chris and the company he was working for with little value, and of course, deals were becoming highly competitive and price driven. Chris is one determined individual; he has never been satisfied with OK results and has always sought to improve. I remember sitting in review meetings with Chris after a loss. We would analyze and reflect upon the loss and discuss how he could develop to avoid a loss in the future.

This focus on continuous self-improvement led Chris to become one of the most confident sales professionals I know. He consistently worked to elevate his language and the approach he took toward customer engagement. These efforts helped build the willingness of senior decision-makers to meet with him as their perception of value grew. Nowadays, Chris always begins meetings with niceties and general conversation, which he tailors to the individual he is meeting. He modifies his approach based on the pre-meeting research he has conducted on that person and their organization. Chris then moves into asking elevated questions (again based on his profiling research) focused either on the organization or person he is meeting with, depending on the relationship. Chris has an eloquent way of asking questions that really positions him as a person of confidence and value.

One joint meeting I had with Chris was with the Chief Information Officer of one of Australia's largest distribution organizations, a decision-maker who I had heard from other salespeople was notoriously tough to deal with and never changed supplier. I knew Chris had conducted robust pre-meeting profiling on this individual and their organization. I knew he was prepared, but I was still nervous about the meeting. I needn't have worried. During this meeting, I observed Chris use elevated quality questions initially around the individual and then the organization. This questioning helped him build rapport and a professional consultative perception in the customer's mind.

Chris demonstrated courtesy by starting the meeting with general talk and niceties. He then moved into questioning, starting with phrases such as "Do you mind sharing something about your background?" "How did you find that?" "What does that look like moving forward?" While asking these questions, Chris was 100% focused on the person he was meeting with. He was seated in a confident, calm manner and asked questions with a level of poise and pace that was highly professional. Many meetings and a few presentations later, Chris won this business, which was worth millions of dollars for his organization. He had successfully built a long-lasting professional relationship with a notoriously tricky decision-maker.

You can continually develop and improve the questions you ask, how you ask them, and your body language. What the customer sees and hears from us is where their perception of us will form and will ultimately play a large part in defining the outcome of the buying journey.

Empathic Listening

In today's world of screen dominance, I believe that we crave face-to-face connection more than ever before. Human connection is a significant emotional driving force from the day we are born and continues throughout our life. We build relationships with our parents and family, friends, our partner, our children, and eventually our grandchildren. In today's world, many of us are gaining our understanding of others through Facebook, Instagram, Twitter, and other social media platforms. Does this information really tell us what is happening, and how people are really feeling? The only way to truly understand someone requires traditional approaches to conversation. I believe that most of us are craving a good conversation with someone who truly cares more than we ever have before.

This is another opportunity for salespeople to really help their customers in line with how customers want to be engaged and helped. As salespeople, we can have conversations with customers that focus on them in a way that today's world is lacking. Empathic listening is the key to showing someone you are genuinely listening and working to understand what they are thinking and feeling. I first learned about empathic listening from Stephen Covey's bestselling book *The 7 Habits of Highly Effective People* (Covey, 1989). It has helped me both personally and in my career. It describes some of the most straightforward skills to be developed and provides the most amazing benefits in life.

The first step to empathic listening is to understand and care about what another person is thinking and feeling. Without the initial desire to do this, it is not worth practicing empathic listening as you will come across as being fake and manipulative. If you do have the desire to truly understand and help someone, you can then practice empathic or active listening as it is also called. The method is simple. All that is required is to focus on the person you are talking to and listen with your ears, eyes, and heart.

With your ears, you are listening what they are saying, trying to truly understand what it is that they are saying and not being biased by your own thinking.

With your eyes, you are observing their body language, hand gestures, and facial expressions. You are trying to capture a broader understanding of what they are thinking.

With your heart, you are using your observations to gain an understanding of what they are feeling at that moment in time.

The final skill of empathic listening is relaying back to the person your understanding of what you heard them say and how you interpreted they feel on this topic. It is this process that demonstrates empathy to another, that you are genuinely listening and trying to understand them.

Empathic listening will provide two key outcomes. Firstly, it will help build a relationship with the other person. The mere fact you are listening, trying to understand them, and demonstrating this through your responses will start to build trust, which is the foundation of any relationship. Secondly, it will provide for a deeper and more meaningful conversation. The act of empathic listening enables corrections of misinterpretation to be made. If what you heard and interpreted is off course, they will correct you. It will also create a safe space for a customer to continue talking on a topic providing you with additional information and a deeper understanding.

Example – Empathic Listening with a Customer

Early on in my sales career, I found myself selling capital equipment for manufacturing sites. I was initially so happy with the promotion to this role and proud of my achievements. This feeling soon vanished when I found myself struggling to deal with decision-makers twice my age with much more experience. I was losing deals and confidence all of the time. A turning point came for me one day in Tasmania. I was engaged in a sales opportunity with a chocolate manufacturer located in Hobart. I was a 23-year-old, barely out of university engaging with a 55-year-old Factory Manager who had worked at the site for 30 plus years. I was thinking to myself, "here we go again." I was on the back foot; this business was a stronghold for a competitor that had been working with them for many years.

I had just read Stephen Covey's book *The 7 Habits of Highly Effective People* (Covey, 1989) for the first time. I decided to practice empathic listening (which I had already had some success with when conversing with my wife). I set up a one-on-one meeting with the Factory Manager. I really focused on understanding him, showing empathy, and finding some areas of relatedness.

Early in the conversation with the Factory Manager, I sensed the stress and pressure he was under with the factory upgrade project he was leading. I heard in his language and saw in his facial expressions and body posture the stress he was feeling. I relayed back to him what I heard him saying and the pressure I sensed he was feeling. This single use of empathic listening sent the conversation in a game-changing direction for me. The Factory Manager opened up about the project and stress he was feeling. I kept using empathic listening to pose back to him what I understood and thought about the different areas of discussion. Every now and then, I got it wrong and was corrected.

The conversation led down a path on how he deals with stress and pressure. I discovered that he loved reading war history books, his favorites being about Albert Jacka, an Australian World War I hero. I also love reading about war history and had just read a book on Albert Jacka that the Factory Manager had not read before. This common interest, along with the empathic conversation, built a high level of connection. Our age difference did not matter. I subsequently express-posted the Albert Jacka book to the Factory Manager so that he could read it on his upcoming flight to England.

We went on to win the business and a lot more over the following years. I believe the level of connection and relationship I formed with the Factory Manager that day and through subsequent meetings played a large part.

Deep Dive on Key Topics

High-level consultants and journalists know how to persist with a line of questioning to uncover a deeper level of truth and understanding. When asking a question, the first response you get will rarely provide the whole picture. Sometimes only a tiny percentage of the total picture is revealed with the first response (Figure 9.3).

It is only the deep dive during questioning that will reveal to you the entire picture. Often you will find this provides a whole new level of understanding. This is not because everyone is trying to hide things from others and give only part of the truth. Typically, the interviewee has never really thought about a specific topic themselves. Your questioning helps you both understand things more deeply, uncovering the bigger picture.

Figure 9.3   Deep-Dive Questioning Iceberg.

Example – Deep Dive

I was working with an organization that sold and serviced industrial automation equipment used within manufacturing and warehouse operations. They were selling the best equipment available in the market, but their sales team were despondent. They had been losing deal after deal because customers were highly focused on the response time to break downs of equipment. My company did not have the service infrastructure of its competitors. They were not in a position to hire more technicians to improve their response time capability.

I conducted some research with the sales team into the current situation and found two key elements:

1. The sales team was mainly dealing with an engineering and maintenance persona.
2. These personas would always raise the topic of how many technicians a potential supplier had and how quickly they could get to site in an emergency.

My first insight was that the sales team was not connecting with higher-level decision-makers.

The second insight came when I asked the sales team, "Why does the customer want to know how many technicians you have and how quickly a technician could get to site when needed?" The only response I got from the team was, "because it's important to them."

I trained and coached the sales team on deep-dive questioning, using words such as "why," "what," and "how" to gain a deeper understanding from the first response a customer provides to a question. I accompanied the team, visiting the maintenance managers to conduct deep-dive questioning on this topic of concern.

We asked the first maintenance manager we met, "Why is service technician response time important to you?" We got the response, "because my manager wants to reduce the downtime of the factory." When we used "why" again to ask, "Why does your manager want to reduce the downtime of the factory?", we got the response, "because it costs a lot if the factory stops producing." We then moved onto a "how" question and asked, "How much does it cost if the factory stops for an hour?" The response was, "I don't know." This questioning had already provided us a more in-depth understanding than we had before. We decided to then meet with the Factory Manager.

The Factory Manager was pleased to meet with us and talk to us on the topic of factory uptime as he called it. This was a vital topic for him. When we asked him, "Why is factory uptime (producing time) so important to you?", he responded, "because it is key to our competitiveness. If the factory goes down even for an hour, the impact is large."

We then asked, "Do you mind telling us how large?" He responded, "Approximately $50,000.00/hour." We immediately understood the scale of the impact. We still continued our deep-dive approach, as we felt there was more to learn about why the competitiveness of the factory is so important right now.

We asked the question, "Why is the competitiveness of the factory so important right now?" We found out that the organization had a sister factory in Indonesia. A threat had been made that if the Australian factory did not improve and become more cost competitive, it would close. One of the most significant impacts on their cost competitiveness was breakdowns that stopped the line running. We asked, "What is the scale of this impact annually?" and found that it was around $10 million.

This example clearly demonstrates the power of deep-dive questioning. The initial position for the sales team was that of losing deals to the competition, who have more technicians and could respond to a breakdown more quickly.

The future state, after gaining a greater understanding through deep-dive questioning, was developing solutions for customers that eliminated breakdowns. This would ensure that their line never broke down with the failure of equipment. The solution they developed provided for a second live backup machine that would kick into gear if the primary unit failed. The cost of the additional equipment was only $15,000.00. The solution saved the site hundreds of thousands a year.

Because the sales team had gained a deeper understanding, they were able to show a payback and ROI based on the downtime the site was incurring, delivering exceptional value and delight to the Factory, Engineering, and Maintenance Manager in the process. The sales team no longer let the sale become about technician response time. Deep-dive questioning enabled them to help decision-makers gain a deeper understanding of the bigger picture and find value in their hot-swap failover solution.

The actual name of this deep-dive questioning approach in Agile is Root Cause Analysis (RCA). We will explore this process briefly so that you understand the process in the event that you are ever asked by a customer who is versed in Agile or Lean.

The 5 Whys or RCA

This technique of questioning is used in many aspects of organization excellence and is commonly called "Root Cause Analysis." The process is focused on reaching the root cause of a situation rather than remaining with the first symptom response to a situation or issue. A simple technique of RCA is the 5 Whys. (There are many other techniques.) This is an approach of asking "why" to a situation several times to find the root cause.

A simple example of this is shown in Figure 9.4.

This example is commonly experienced by salespeople focused on selling to procurement officers and managers. Salespeople dread the response from a customer "Price is essential, and you are off the mark." If your organization is not a price leader, this is a problem. If your salespeople are not skilled at deep-dive questioning, they will find themselves stressed and typically reducing their margins to hopefully win the business.

Deep-dive questioning provides salespeople and customers a simultaneous, more in-depth and elevated understanding. This awareness naturally elevates your sales approach and lifts the customer's perception of the value provided. The technique is one of the most straightforward, practical skills to implement to enhance your researching approach with customers.

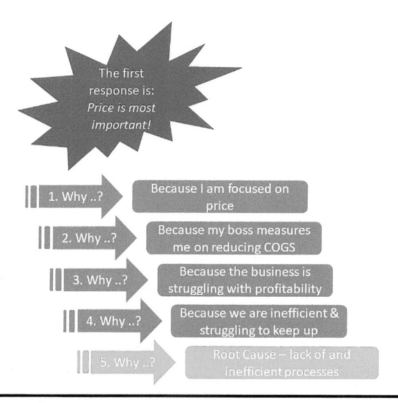

Figure 9.4 5 Whys.

We will now discuss the critical phase of "Purchase," the phase in the customer's buying journey that we all strive to reach and complete to bring our customers further value and delight.

Suggested Actions for "Research"

"Research" is the phase of the buying journey that will make or break you. It is the phase of the buying journey that your customers will build and cement their perception of yourself and your organization.

The following suggested actions will help you elevate this perception:

1. Choose an approach to pre-plan your sales meetings.
2. Practice elevating your conversation with a teammate or your leader. Role-play a discussion about the persona's background, direction, and challenges. Then role-play a conversation about their organization's background, direction, and challenges. Practice using empathic listening as part of these role plays.

3. Test the use of "why" or "what" questions to gain a deeper understanding with a teammate or a customer's initial responses to questions.
4. Put the techniques into practice in your sales calls. Use the pre-planning techniques to help you plan and think about your call and the new methods you want to practice ahead of time.
5. Rate yourself on these skills after each sale call (one: no-good, two: OK, three: good). Note down ways by which you think you could improve next time, and practice these ideas before your next customer meeting.

These steps will elevate your customer's perception of you and your company. This elevated perception will help you in moving more sales to the "Purchase" phase and with more margin.

Chapter 10

Purchase

This is the phase of the customer's buying journey that we all want to be a part of! The approach we take during the "Discovery" and "Research" phases of the buying journey is crucial in determining our success in continuing forward with a purchase.

There is an old saying in sales that "To get a customer to purchase, the pain of the change needs to be less than the pain of the same." The sales game is all about change. Every time we achieve sales success, we have taken a customer through change. The customer has purchased a new or changed item or service. They have committed to implementing an improvement solution with us, or they have purchased a completely new system. Change always brings with it risks and difficulties which decision-making personas understand. These factors create the pain of change, which every salesperson battles with to win a deal.

There are four areas I would like to introduce to help a sales organization limit the pain of change and amplify the motivation for a customer to move forward with them:

1. Simplify the purchase.
2. Motivate the purchase.
3. Lead the journey to purchase.
4. Close with abundance.

These elements will help a customer move into and through purchasing with value and delight. This will ultimately assist the sales organization in achieving greater success and growth. They can be challenging areas to improve. I will provide tips and tricks together with case studies on these that will help you and your team move forward.

Simplify the "Purchase"

Why do organizations make it more difficult to purchase than it should be? I am sure we have all experienced having to fill out copious forms to make a purchase, waiting while a salesperson gets their technology system working or standing in queues waiting to buy. Sales and marketing team members have worked so hard to get a customer to the "Purchase" phase of their buying journey, and then we proceed to make it painful.

The other frustrating experience for sales professionals is, when asking for the order, hearing dreaded responses that form a barrier to the purchase. These include responses such as following from the decision-maker:

- I need to think about it.
- The timing is not right.
- I have a budget constraint.

I pose to you that these responses are not reality. The reality is that decision-makers (if you have gotten to them) are not motivated enough to purchase. If they were motivated enough, they would not be thinking about it or concerned about timing. They would find a way around budget constraints and not give you flippant responses like "I need to think about it."

Let's explore how to limit barriers to purchase.

Limit Barriers to "Purchase"

We have all experienced the simple journey of downloading a free app from an app store. This is one of the simplest and most common purchases which employ limited barriers. These apps generate additional revenue through advertising, upgrades, and accepting the use of the full edition automatically after a period. If you are a successful app developer, keep up the excellent work! If you keep improving to stay ahead of your competition, you probably won't gain value from this section. I speculate that most of you are not purely app developers and will be looking for ways to limit barriers to purchase and achieve more sales.

Where do barriers to purchase come from? They are typically imposed by bureaucracy within our own organizations. Why do we impose internal systems and procedures that make it more difficult for customers to purchase from us?

I have had these debates with many accounting and finance teams over the years, and these reasons spring to mind:

■ Legal obligations.
■ Risk mitigation.
■ That's our process.
■ Stop wasting my time and go and sell more.

The same people who build such barriers to purchase within our organizations are typically the ones handling the money and getting stressed about how much we are selling! I know this is a highly frustrating position to be in as salespeople and sales leaders. Believe me, I have been there many times, looking at these colleagues in disbelief.

Creating a Holistic, Agile Organization

Creating an Agile organization is the key to overcoming these cultural and process barriers. The introduction to Agile Sales I provided earlier in this book is a starting point when contemplating the different approaches. Organizations who achieve excellence in these areas are on an Agile journey as a whole. Yes, accounts receivable, delivery, and finance teams are focused on improving the buying journey for their customers. They all:

■ Understand internal and external customer value and delight,
■ Align and engage in innovation,
■ Run rapid, Agile improvement meetings (Scrums),
■ Have visual measures and improvement boards to drive continual improvement and innovation with the customer front and center to the process, and
■ Are actively leading and coaching the journey.

Although Agile is the right approach for the market we now find ourselves in, there are still people who don't care and don't want to change. As an organization improvement consultant, I come across these people every day of my life. I have developed a few techniques that have helped the organizations that I work for. Here are my tips.

Understand Your Internal Customers

An internal customer is a person or team within your organization who is the next step in the process of delivering value to an external customer. Considering a sales process, our internal customers are typically the finance, accounts receivable, project delivery, manufacturing, and supply chain teams. It is also these teams that we feel create barriers to a smooth and easy sale. The concept of understanding your external customers and key personas can equally be applied to knowing your internal customers. Try putting yourself in their shoes. Take the time to truly understand them and why they have built these barriers for you and the external customer. Once you recognize their world, you will be in a better position to engage them in the right way to achieve change and ultimately help your external customer. You may even begin to understand and change some things that you and your sales team do. This will help things to flow more smoothly for your internal customers (finance, production, supply chain).

Take Them to See

Another approach I find really works is taking your internal customers to see great practice in a similar organization. You may know of a local company that has made improvements in your area of focus, which would open their doors and show you both how they operate and the journey they took to achieve this. Helping others to see great practice in action is a lot more powerful than just talking about it. The saying that "seeing is believing" is so true. One point of caution: ensure that you do your research on the organization and people you are taking them to ahead of time. The other place you can take challenging internal customers to see is your external customers. Taking internal customers out to see external customers, live in their shoes, and learn is an excellent step to overcoming paradigms that hinder improvement to make things simpler.

Involve Them in Customer Journey Mapping

The final option I would like to highlight is involving your internal customers in a customer journey mapping event. This is a process of mapping a current persona's journey through "Discovery," "Research," "Purchase," "Delivery," and "Devotion" with your organization. The method provides a cross-functional team with the opportunity to live in the customer's shoes and look at their experience with your organization from the customer's perspective. There are many firms around the world, including my own, that will help an organization map this process. We aim to define an improved future state journey to work toward to deliver customers higher value and delight. I recommend conducting this mapping as part of your organizational strategic and financial planning approach.

Example – Signet, Customer Journey Mapping

Signet has a fantastic approach toward improving its customer's buying journey, led by Signet's Customer Experience Leader, Rufaro Mtuwa. As part of their 2018 strategic planning, Rufaro formed a cross-functional team of influential stakeholders. She believed this team considering the whole supply chain/value stream, would help her achieve a better experience for their customers.

The team initially analyzed its customer data. They utilized the Pareto Principle to gain an understanding of who the customers to whom they delivered the most value were. Then they conducted "customer service safaris" to truly understand the primary decision-making personas within these organizations. They discovered a critical decision-making persona they named "Barry." They were able to uncover a lot of crucial information about "Barry" and used this as the focus of their customer journey mapping.

They mapped "Barry"'s typical buying journey, from "Discovery" through to "Devotion" with Signet. They explored what "Barry" does at each of these stages when engaging with Signet, what questions he has at each step, and how he feels considering the current experience. What resulted was a current state journey map (Figure 10.1) that the team used to generate further ideas and opportunities for improvement.

Using a PICK (possible, implement, challenge, kill) chart, the team ranked the improvement ideas generated by the level of improvement they would provide for "Barry," and how easy or hard they were to implement. Prioritized improvement areas were then captured in the relevant strategic planning documents and executed as part of team RVMs (rapid visual meetings) over the coming year. The results have been amazing: quality

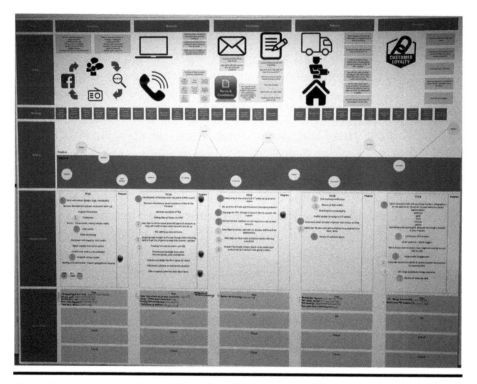

Figure 10.1   Customer Journey Map, Signet.

improvements up to 99.99%, a net promoter score of over 69%, and a qua-drupling in organic sales growth.

Improvements that were implemented from Signet's customer journey mapping efforts helped. More importantly, I believe that the cross-functional awareness and culture change that resulted played an even more significant part in achieving improvement in results for the business and for "Barry"!

Motivate the "Purchase"

Senior decision-makers make decisions based on data. They typically love dollar savings and percentage gains. They don't like promises and pitches about features and benefits. What they care about is the results the change will give them and how they will help them move toward achieving their goals.

Salespeople who are not skilled at capturing data and presenting it to senior decision-makers create the following two adverse outcomes for themselves:

1. The customer working out the returns themselves (which is risky, as they are not an expert in your solutions) or
2. No one working out the returns and the deal dying because senior decision-makers did not understand the value.

Senior decision-making personas are typically risk-averse; they will stay with the "pain of the same" if they can't clearly quantify the gains. Quantifying gains from a solution should be done by the solution expert in collaboration with the customer. If you leave it to the customer to quantify the gains, you risk the calculation of incorrect figures, which are typically underestimated. These results won't give decision-makers correct data on payback or return on investment (ROI).

I believe the salesperson and their subject matter experts are in the best position to collaborate with customers. Together they can calculate gains from a solution and the resulting payback and ROI figures.

This process will provide quality information that enables senior decision-making personas to:

- Rapidly make a decision to move forward or not and
- Quickly discover if there is no payback or ROI, allowing you to terminate the project quickly rather than wasting further time.

Both outcomes are a win: a faster deal when the payback and ROI add up and reduced time wasted when they don't. You may be thinking, "Brad, I don't agree with this. I don't want my customers knowing the payback or ROI, as it may not be good enough for them, and they may not buy because of this."

Believe it or not, I have found that having a clear agreed-upon payback or ROI for a solution speeds up the purchase process by 35% and improves a team's closing rate by 20%. Selling with abundance is about selling to help customers improve and overcome challenges. It is about being transparent and to the point. Calculating payback and ROI with a customer is living the abundant approach. The statistics prove that you will win more deals and close deals more quickly in the process.

How to Calculate Payback

Payback = Total cost of the solution ÷ annualized returns from the solution.

Calculate the total fixed cost of your solution for the customer and then the new or additional ongoing costs they will incur, such as consumables, maintenance, training, etc. Note the fixed costs as a once-off cost and the reoccurring costs/year separately as an ongoing rolling cost for one, two, three, and four years after the sale. Calculate the annualized returns from your solution as comprehensively as you can. Think about cost reductions, time savings resulting in reduced labor requirements or overtime costs, defect/quality savings, safety gains reducing related costs, absenteeism reduction, and additional profits from greater throughput/ speed capabilities. These savings are typically ongoing; chart them in a rolling trend line for one, two, three, and four years after the solution is installed.

Payback is simply the time it takes for an investment to pay for itself from the returns it generates. This is typically shown in years, for example, half a year payback or three and a half years payback.

Let's work through an example of payback.

Fixed solution costs: The cost of the new solution, including once-off installation and training,

is $50,000.00.

Ongoing new costs: Ongoing maintenance cost is $2,000.00/year.

Direct savings: The solution will save $10,000.00 in consumable spend/ year and $60,000.00 in labor.

Payback formula is:

$52,000.00 ÷ $70,000.00 = **0.74 years**.

A great way to display this visually is by using a waterfall chart (Figure 10.2).

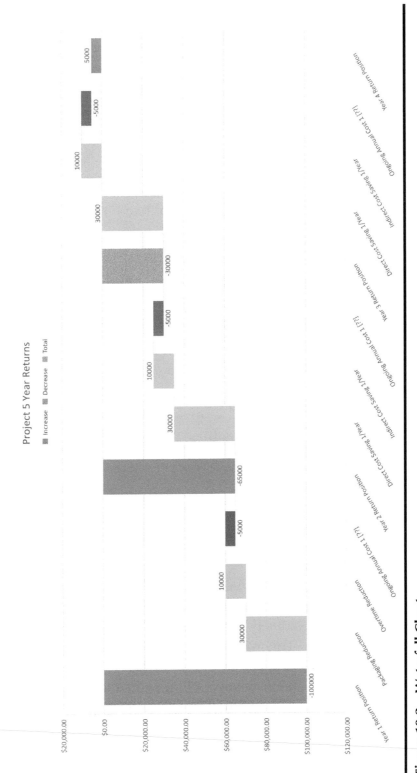

Figure 10.2 Waterfall Chart.

How to Calculate ROI

ROI is a formula that enables the returns on an investment to be predicted at a specified future date. To develop an ROI, a period (usually expressed in number of years) should be specified for the calculation, for example, one year or five years. Alternatively, you can show the ROI for several years, for example, the first, second, third, and fourth years after investment.

> The formula for ROI is:
>   Profit or return from an investment ÷ Initial fixed investment.

The resulting figure is shown as a percentage.

You are looking for the difference between the returns from an investment and the initial investment plus ongoing costs after the specified period. This calculation will give you the estimated profit from the investment; you then divide the estimated profit by the initial fixed investment cost to get your ROI percentage.

> Let's use the previous example (used above for payback) this ROI example.
>   We will calculate ROI after one year.
>   Profit after one year: $70,000.00 (Returns) – $52,000.00 (Investment cost) = $18,000.00.
>   Return on investment after one year = $18,000.00 ÷ $52,000.00 = **34.6%**.
>   The figure (34.6%) represents the percentage of the initial investment returned through predicted profitable gains after one year.

Please note that every customer will have a different view on what is a good or lousy payback and similarly, ROI. Work with the financial decision-makers of your customers early on in the process to appreciate their standards in this area. This will help you understand if the deal is worth pursuing early on, saving you time and hassle.

I have spoken a lot about consultative selling with abundance throughout this book. I now want to discuss how you can use your knowledge and expertise in your field to build tension, helping to motivate and move buyers through the "Purchase" phase. We are going to explore selling with abundant confidence in this section.

Build Buying Tension through Commercial Storytelling

Commercial storytelling is very similar to the storytelling coaching technique I outlined earlier in this book. Many of our world's largest organizations have used it extensively in education, sharing knowledge and creating change. It plays directly to the way our minds want to be communicated with, visually with emotion. Consider a movie you love. Did this movie create vivid pictures for you and trigger an emotional reaction? Did you relate to the story of this movie in some way? Did it inspire you, and motivate you to make a change? Our minds are fine-tuned to take in information as stories and their related images. If we relate to these stories and they trigger our emotions, we are even more captivated. Commercial storytelling is a powerful way of conveying insights and solutions to help customers understand what we are presenting, agree to our proposition, and move forward with the purchase.

Commercial storytelling:

1. Is focused
2. Is future-oriented and vivid
3. Provides facts and figures
4. Creates forward motion

The story will create a vision for the future that motivates a customer to move forward with the sales process. I call the approach the "4Fs" of telling a compelling commercial story (Figure 10.3).

Focus

Focus the conversation by clarifying with empathy a key concern, or goal for the customer, and how you interpret their feelings about it. This allows you to focus the customer's attention and ensure you are on the same page of understanding. It also instantly builds relatedness for the customer as you are highlighting an area of importance for them that you are about to tell a commercial story. This step enables you to lead the conversation, focusing on a critical area of importance to the customer where you can most effectively help them. Wherever possible, focus and align the conversation to the unique capabilities of your organization. Highlighting concerns or goals a customer has raised with you in a way that moves the story toward areas of competitive advantage is always a good move. Commercial storytelling is to

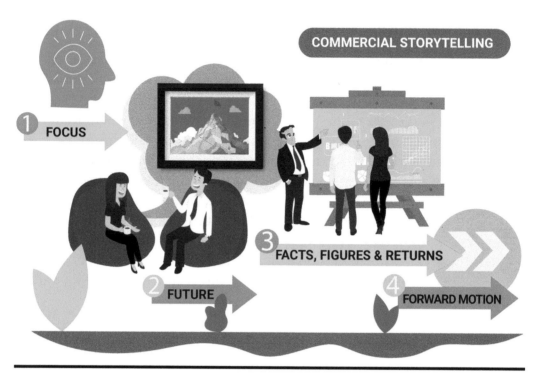

Figure 10.3 Commercial Storytelling.

the point and takes a few minutes max. To achieve this, you need to focus on the conversation and build relatedness quickly.

Future

The future is where your story starts. We are all tuned to focusing on the future rather than dwelling in the past. In discussing the future, create a vivid picture in the customer's mind that helps them to understand what could be achieved. This will also help the customer to lock it into their memory and build emotional motivation about what could be achieved.

A vivid picture requires context. The context (meaning, setting, background) of the story may be describing a similar case example with a related client that your customer can relate to. Or it could be painting a clear picture of how things would look, perform, and feel in the future with your help.

A vivid picture also requires texture, which is created by using location and building emotion/tension in the story. Let's talk about location first. The more you can place your story about the future in a place or location, describing what it would be like, the more memorable it will be. This could be to detail the situation and physical position of the case example.

You could mention what the future would look like at a specific time and place when you meet after the improvement has been implemented. The human brain is tuned to memorize data linked to locational information. Most people can remember where they were when substantial events occurred but have difficulty remembering many other details.

The second factor is bringing emotion/tension into the story about the future. A moderate level of emotion helps strengthen information in our minds. If you have a commercial story that incorporates both negative and positive tension/emotion for the customer, start with the negative elements and finish with the positive. Negative emotion grabs the customer's attention but can also paralyze them if you are not careful. This is why you always follow with positive emotional factors. We are wired to move toward the positive, and this is what we want the customer to do with us through their buying journey.

As an example, using the related case approach, you describe the client you've worked with, highlighting the areas of relatedness to the customer. You tell the story of the challenges they faced and the concerns they had for their future. You mention how these risks are similar to those confronting your client right now. You then tell the tale of how you overcame these challenges and the resulting gains the client achieved. You describe how the situation looked and progressed and the positive impact it had on the customer and their team. This style of storytelling has the client visualizing the future with a decent level of emotional connection. It is now time to bring in the facts and figures.

Facts, Figures, and Returns

Senior leaders make decisions based on facts, figures, and returns. These particulars give decision-makers what they want to hear. They also validate the commercial story you are telling and build motivation to move forward. If you have done some initial analysis on payback and ROI, you have facts and figures available to bring into your story. If not, your related case examples may have returns and percentage gains and savings that you can share. Even though these figures are not specific, a relevant case example providing facts and figures will help validate your story and build motivation to move forward. Related reports and studies are also a great place to draw facts and figures from for use in commercial stories. Studies have been conducted on most things, providing a great source of supporting information and statistics. Simply google topics of relevance to the challenges and goals you help your customers with; you will be surprised with what you find.

Forward Motion – Next Steps

Forward motion is all about leading the buying journey toward the next steps as part of your commercial story. You must have clarity of these next steps and deliver these with confidence. You have just created a vivid picture of what the future could look like for your customer. You have brought in both negative and positive emotions, backed by facts and figures, to help motivate them to progress. Now it is time to ensure forward motion continues by outlining the next steps and gaining their agreement to move forward. The more you can bring structure into your commercial storytelling, particularly with forward movement, or next steps, the more success you will have. Sales resources that provide visuals for the customer and the next steps can really help. The following case example from Signet will highlight this approach.

Example: Commercial Storytelling, Signet

Signet built a great commercial storytelling approach focused on supply chain load containment. Typically, pallets of goods being transported are wrapped in plastic (pallet wrap) to secure the load for transportation. This process is critical to ensuring safety during storage, as pallets are often located many stories up in a warehouse. If a carton fell from that height, anyone standing under it could be seriously injured, and it could cause massive damage to the products inside of the carton. Similarly, pallets in trucks, boats, planes, and trains are at risk if they move or shift. Unstable pallets lead to damaged goods. They can also lead to transportation accidents caused by the shifting of weight within the vehicle.

Signet sales staff often discover clients not wrapping pallets correctly. When they identify this, a commercial story is presented at the right time in the sales process that incorporates both negative and positive tension. They focus the conversation initially on clarifying what they saw, or the customer said, and how they believe the customer feels about this. Please note the customer may not be concerned at this stage. They then present a future picture that defines the hidden costs of load containment. They tailor their story to the customer and their industry. They highlight how this relates to what the customer is most focused on strategically and culturally, i.e. environment, safety, quality. They paint a picture of the possible future risks (Figure 10.4) and then quickly move to the gains (Figure 10.5).

They discuss examples they have seen and worked on in the past, how the improved system looked, and what the team experienced as part of this process. They draw on appropriate facts and figures, outlining the potential gains from the improvement and, again, referencing relevant case examples.

The Hidden Costs of Poor Load Containment

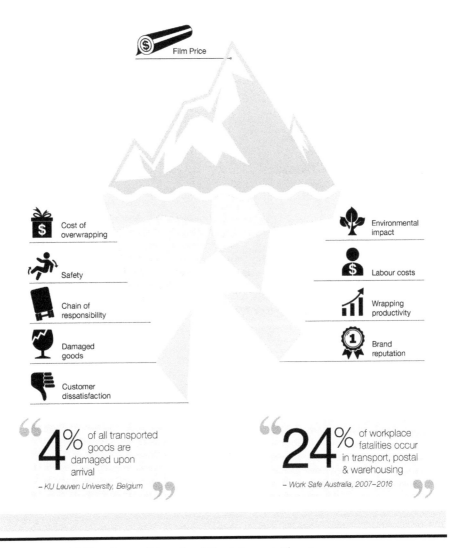

Film Price

Cost of overwrapping

Safety

Chain of responsibility

Damaged goods

Customer dissatisfaction

Environmental impact

Labour costs

Wrapping productivity

Brand reputation

4% of all transported goods are damaged upon arrival
– *KU Leuven University, Belgium*

24% of workplace fatalities occur in transport, postal & warehousing
– *Work Safe Australia, 2007–2016*

Figure 10.4   Hidden Costs of Poor Load Containment, Signet.

The decision-making personas hearing this compelling commercial story are taken on a journey. Through the negative aspects of the unfolding story, backed by facts and figures, they are thinking, "Wow, that could happen to us" or "Is it occurring now, and I don't know about it?"

Tertiary Optimisation Results

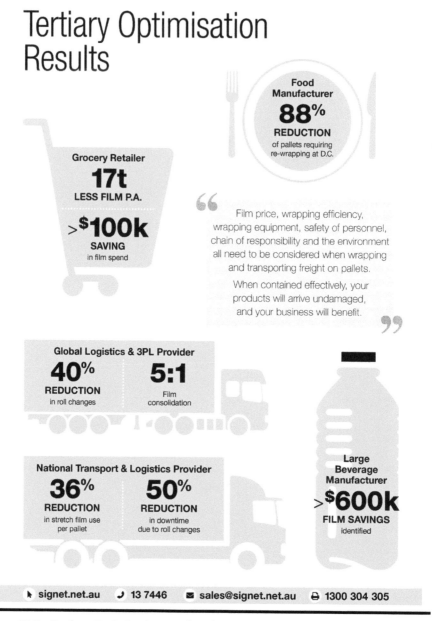

Grocery Retailer
17t
LESS FILM P.A.

>**$100k**
SAVING
in film spend

Food Manufacturer
88%
REDUCTION
of pallets requiring re-wrapping at D.C.

" Film price, wrapping efficiency, wrapping equipment, safety of personnel, chain of responsibility and the environment all need to be considered when wrapping and transporting freight on pallets.

When contained effectively, your products will arrive undamaged, and your business will benefit. "

Global Logistics & 3PL Provider
40%
REDUCTION
in roll changes

5:1
Film consolidation

National Transport & Logistics Provider
36%
REDUCTION
in stretch film use per pallet

50%
REDUCTION
in downtime due to roll changes

Large Beverage Manufacturer
>**$600k**
FILM SAVINGS
identified

▸ signet.net.au ✆ 13 7446 ✉ sales@signet.net.au 🖶 1300 304 305

Figure 10.5   Tertiary Optimization Results, Signet.

With the positive side of the future story, they are thinking, "Wow, there are some good commercial, quality, and safety gains to achieve out of this. We need to make this happen!"

The statistics and case examples have the customer thinking, "This has an upside. Some of our competitors have taken advantage of this already and captured these gains. We need to keep up."

This commercial story example from Signet builds energy and motivation within the customer to move forward. The technique and sales tools create vivid, relatable pictures in the customer's mind, enhanced by emotion and validated by facts and figures. Customers are ready to move forward; they want to hear the next steps and get moving. It is essential for any sales organization that this path forward plays directly into their unique areas of capability to ensure competitive advantage. We will explore this topic in the next section.

Quote Nashis, Not Apples

The key to quoting, which is an essential step in the buying journey, is to sustain your point of difference. Being able to differentiate your quotation amplifies in importance when a procurement manager is a decision-maker. Price-sensitive personas want to compare apples with apples. They want a quote for apples from a few different companies so that they can commoditize the deal and apply pressure on the price to negotiate the best outcome possible. This is an excellent procurement negotiation tactic and delivers results. Many salespeople get caught in this trap. They are so excited to be able to quote a particular item for a customer that they quickly form up and submit a quote purely for the apple.

While researching procurement personas, we have found a common trait. They will show interest in a quotation if it is at least 5%–10% cheaper. If a current supplier is doing a satisfactory job, they will not change. Procurement personas will let their current supplier know they have received a lower price and use this as leverage to negotiate them down. This procurement persona behavior saves time and mitigates risk. They know the current supplier and potentially have some form of relationship with them. If a procurement persona is changing their supplier, they are taking a risk. Staying with the existing supplier and getting the benefit of a lower price is a quick low-risk win.

A nashi is an Asian pear that looks a lot like an apple. It is unique and tastes incredible (to me anyway). It closely resembles an apple but has other unique characteristics that differentiate it. When quoting, we need to quote nashis, not apples, to motivate the purchase, highlight our points of difference, and sustain/create a competitive advantage.

First of all, identify the uniqueness of your offering and capabilities. You may produce and sell a commoditized product, but what else does your organization do uniquely? What could you bundle into your quotations to create a nashi rather than an apple? Here are some examples:

1. Unique brand names for products
2. Unique offerings that can be bundled together, such as free telephone support for items you sell
3. Broad solution ranges, such as consumables, hardware, and service, that are different from competitors
4. Unique knowledge and skills, technical experts, or subject matter experts that can be used to deliver higher value to a customer
5. Unique services such as recycling support options for customers that your competitors are not currently offering.

Unique offerings must be valued by the customer. The profiling that you complete throughout the "Research" phase of the buying journey will help you achieve this. When creating a quote for a nashi that includes unique offerings, do not break out individual pricing for each item; price it as one complete bundle. This helps you sustain the nashi by not allowing it to be turned back into an apple. It also provides you power if the buying journey moves into a negotiation phase.

If you have provided a customer with a quote that includes four other bundled elements of value, you are in a strong negotiating position. The buying persona can clearly see the value you offer in the quotation. (Many buyers won't read a full proposal; they go straight to the quote.) If the buyer starts putting pressure on you with pricing, trying to compare you to one of the other quotes for apples they have received, always show empathy to their request first. Then ask them what they would like removed from the quotation. You are willing to negotiate, but an area of value is going to be removed to compensate for the price reduction. Through this process, you can provide the customer insights as to the importance of the additional items, applying respectful, consultative pressure on their decision. We will explore this approach further in handling objections with abundance later in this book.

Leading the Journey to "Purchase"

Usually, there are only three options for who the leader of the buying journey is: the customer, the salesperson, or no one! Of course, we don't want to get to the place where no one is leading the buying journey and the deal has died. But who should lead the journey? Traditionally, it has been the customer who leads their own buying journey with salespeople competing to gain the customer's decision to buy. Is there a better way? Would it help a salesperson if they could lead the journey?

According to the typical voice of customer information that I have outlined, we find that customers are asking for help to solve their problems and achieve their goals. Customers are seeking help, and due to this, I pose that there is an opportunity for the salesperson to lead the buying journey. The results of the consultations I have completed with organizations support this. The highest performing sales teams have two traits. The first is the ability to elevate the customer's perception of the value and delight they can offer. The second is the ability to lead the buying journey. I have seen organizations achieve upward of 70% sales improvement year on year through a shift in their approach on both scales.

The Sales Excellence Maturity Index

The sales maturity index (Figure 10.6) is based on two analysis elements

1. Ability to lead the buying journey
2. The value and delight perception developed within buying personas.

The left-hand column defines the different levels of ability for a sales team to lead the buying journey. The right-hand column shows the differing levels of value and delight a sales team can build with their customers. It is a simple model; progressing up its levels will help you and your sales team grow dramatically in sales performance. Let's explore each level of the maturity index.

The lowest level of sales team performance sits around the reactive approach to leading the customer's buying journey and vendor perception. At this stage of maturity, a sales team does not have a structured approach to leading a customer's buying journey. They are typically selling based on product, supply, and price. This is the lowest level of performance because sales teams selling at this level of maturity are selling a commodity without any real process to deliver higher value to a customer.

A team that develops a process to lead a customer's buying journey with value, and sells based on unique solutions, will elevate themselves to the next level of performance (level 2). The salespeople in the team act as value-added consultants. They differentiate themselves from the reactive vendor

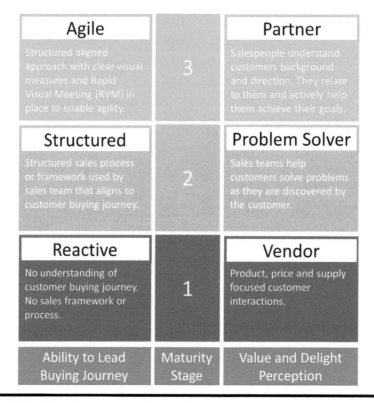

Figure 10.6 Sales Excellence Maturity Index.

sales approach by offering additional value and a structured approach to help their customers move through the buying journey.

Reaching level 3 of the maturity index is more difficult but not impossible. It requires a sales organization to become skilled at profiling its customer's personal and organizational background, strategic direction, and challenges. Salespeople operating at this level of maturity can engage senior decision-making personas at elevated levels. They can clearly demonstrate how their business aligns with the customer's background and culture. They expertly help the customer overcome challenges and achieve their strategic direction.

Level 3 involves a sales organization becoming proficient at many of the Agile Sales foundational approaches such as Hoshin Kanri, Scrum, Kanban, and Sprints. These Agile skills bring a level of speed and agility to a sales organization. The business can flex and adjust quickly when required to get a deal over the line and continuously innovate and improve to sustain their point of difference. A sales organization that reaches level 3 is doing exceptionally well.

It is challenging for the competition to ever catch a sales team operating at level 3 due to the continuous innovation that is occurring. The competition may strive to reach them; they may set a target and work on reaching that target over several years. The issue they face is that a sales organization operating at level 3 is not stationary. They continue to improve and innovate for those years also, always keeping themselves several years ahead of their competition.

Sales Process Aligned to the Customer's Journey

To have any chance of reaching level 3 of the Agile Sales excellence maturity index, a sales organization needs to develop a structured value-added process to engage and consult with its customers. Please note the sales approach I am talking about is not the traditional pain/feature benefits approach we have been training salespeople in for years. The process I am referring to is a systematic consultative approach aligned to the customer's buying journey. The approach is designed to take a customer through their buying journey, helping them overcome challenges and achieve their strategic direction.

The following three tips will help a sales organization develop a structured approach:

1. Understand the Sprint scientific thinking approach to improvement. Developing a valuable consultative approach to help customers requires an organization to initially understand best practices in continuous improvement (CI). You can't help a customer improve effectively if your team does not understand the fundamentals of CI. If your organization is on an Agile journey and adopting these best practice techniques, I recommend developing your team initially on the systematic Sprint approach to improvement. Plan–Do–Check–Act (PDCA) is a brilliant scientific thinking approach to CI. Another improvement approach to explore is the Define, Measure, Analyze, Improve, Control (DMAIC) system used in Six Sigma. Understanding these approaches, some of the history, and why they have been successful will help provide your sales team with the skills and ability to develop and adopt a consultative CI sales process.
2. Define the unique knowledge, skills, techniques, and offerings your organization has.
   I have never met a sales team that did not have some unique areas of knowledge, skills, techniques, and offerings for customers. Sometimes

these unique capabilities sit with only a few of the team members, typically the highest performers. It is essential to capture and document these and build everyone's knowledge and awareness of these. Current and potential unique areas of expertise and capability can be brainstormed, defined, and then used as part of a customer journey mapping event.

3. Use customer journey mapping to develop your sales process. Customer journey mapping, which we have previously covered, is an excellent tool and technique to identify improvement opportunities for customer-facing processes such as sales. By mapping a customer's buying journey, a sales team can place themselves in the customer's shoes and define a process and key measures to track performance through the "Discovery," "Research," and "Purchase" phases of the journey. Start by mapping the customer's journey through this process. Ask the team how a customer would ultimately like the buying journey to flow. Map your customer-facing (sales and marketing) process to define an approach to help them through this journey with value and delight.

Selling Toilet Paper with Value

There are not many products more commoditized than toilet paper! I could have won some money betting that salespeople could sell toilet paper in a consultative value-added way. I am not a gambling man and would rather share with you how far the creation of a consultative value-adding sales approach can go. Let's explore the case study on this topic of selling toilet paper with abundance.

> **Example: Signet, Selling Toilet Paper with Value**
>
> Signet has been on the sales excellence journey for many years, and hygiene systems are one of the many areas in which Signet helps its customers. Signet developed a value-adding sales approach, aligned to their customer's buying journey to help elevate their value perception with customers and start leading the buying journey with value and delight.
>
> Signet had an existing culture of CI, having been on a Lean CI journey internally for many years. The shift to this value-adding sales approach was not a significant one for the company to make. A central team involving different team members from all levels of the organization was formed to explore their unique capabilities (knowledge, skills, techniques, and offerings). They then mapped a process to define a value-adding sales approach. The team built a process based on the PDCA approach to CI (Figure 10.7).

The team found that they had extensive knowledge of hygiene systems and safety, covering many different industries and years of experience. The group pooled this knowledge and developed some best-practice approaches supported by documentation and training materials.

Major manufacturers and logistics companies were the focus areas for the new process. These organizations see bathroom cleanliness and hygiene as key to health and safety. Through this new approach, the Signet sales team were able to elevate their conversations around site safety and hygiene with senior decision-making personas. They were able to provide insights to these decision-makers around the impact of poorly maintained bathrooms and general area toilets on employees and team culture. These decision-makers valued the conversation and knowledge supplied by Signet. They allowed the sales team to work through their safety and hygiene optimization program with them. In doing so, they invited the Signet sales team to lead the buying journey and deliver them excellent value.

As with all systematic improvement approaches, the process is not complicated. The Signet sales team use the knowledge they have gained through profiling the customer and decision-makers to identify opportunities to help them in their areas of expertise. They meet with these decision-makers to

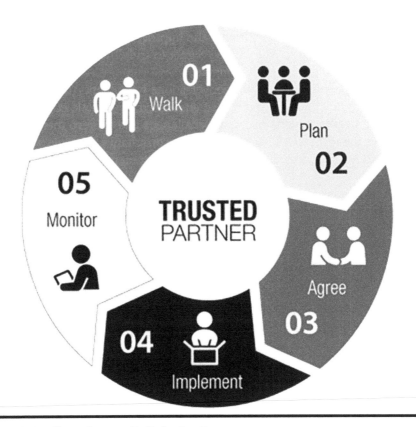

Figure 10.7   Signet Process Optimization Program.

gain a deeper understanding of their background, direction, and challenges both personally and from an organization perspective. They then conduct a walk through the customer's operations with several key decision-making personas and front-line leaders. During the walk, when an improvement opportunity is identified, they will probe in depth to understand the root causes of what is currently occurring. This elevates the customer's understanding of the situation. When they are asked "why?" or "what causes this?" several times, they understand the bigger picture. The team then ask, "How much is this costing you?" As this question follows the bigger picture (the customer has discovered the seriousness of the situation), an accurate return can be estimated.

Following the walk, they move into planning, prioritizing the improvements with the decision-makers using a PICK (possible, implement, challenge, kill) chart (covered in Chapter 5). More in-depth planning may or may not be required following this, depending on the scale and complexity of the improvement. If it is a simple improvement and the key stakeholders are present, they will prompt agreement by discussing the next steps for the prioritized improvement.

Implementation for simple improvements can be as easy as setting a date to implement or pilot the improvement. The team will then monitor the improvement to ensure it achieves the returns predicted. If the gains are not achieved, they will simply go through the improvement cycle again. This structured CI approach to sales allows Signet to truly live its purpose and help its customers improve and compete.

Signet salespeople elevate their conversations with clients, understand the value that they provide, and have a structured, systematic continuous approach to help customers overcome challenges and achieve their goals. This allows the team to sell toilet paper in a consultative strategic way, delivering fantastic value and delight to their customers.

Close with Abundance

Why is it that so many salespeople struggle to close? I believe it is because of traditional low-value sales techniques focused on finding the pain and selling on product features and benefits (levels 1 and 2 of the sales excellence maturity index). At this level of sales approach, there is typically a low level of value perceived by the customer who is entirely in control of the buying journey.

As a sales team reaches level 3 of the sales excellence maturity index, they are selling with greater value and delight. They are targeting senior decision-makers with value; they are leading the buying journey and are in a strong position to close. Their structured consultative approach allows them to lead the buying journey. This includes an agreement phase: a stage in the process where the sale can be confirmed to move forward or not. I call this stage the check-in.

Check-In

The check-in aligns with the "Purchase" phase of a customer's buying journey. It involves linking with all the senior decision-makers to review the data gained through the process so far and consider the proposed future state. The check-in is a simple three-step process (Figure 10.8).

Background Alignment

The consultative sales approach provides the sales team with a fantastic alignment to present at this stage of the buying journey. The team can show relatedness and alignment with personal and organizational background and culture (as discovered in the "Research" phase). This approach to alignment helps build relatedness and supports the relationship and confidence that decision-making personas have in you and your company.

Direction Alignment

Direction alignment is all about demonstrating how you can help the decision-makers, and their organization, achieve strategic direction and goals now and into the future. Direction alignment maintains the elevated approach to business dealings and aligns yourself and your organization

 Background Alignment

 Direction Alignment

 Move Forward?

Figure 10.8   Check-In Process.

with what is most important to senior decision-makers. Presenting directional alignment will help you prioritize your work with the customer and determine the value they perceive in you and your organization. Direction alignment is your time to present the future state, potential gains, payback, and how this will help your customer strategically. You can also reinforce some of the key insights you have provided them so far throughout the buying journey and how these align with where they are going into the future.

Move Forward

The final step of the check-in is asking, "Are we right to move forward with the next step of the process?" which will be either a purchase or pilot. There are two outcomes you will receive at this stage: a simple "yes" or an objection. Of course, if you get a "yes," you are moving into "Delivery." If you get a "no," you are into handling an objection (to be covered soon).

Salespeople need to be skilled at asking a closed probe at this point, ensuring they get a yes or no from the customer. I have covered the need for open probes through the "Research" phase of the buying journey, but that does not apply when you are closing. I teach every salesperson I deal with to always ask for the order! I must admit that this is one of the most common weaknesses I find when coaching salespeople. Partly this is caused by traditional low-value sales approaches; salespeople have been shot down so many times in the past that they learn to avoid asking for the order.

If a salesperson has helped a customer through their buying journey with value and delight, they are in a strong position to ask for the order. This must be done with abundance and confidence. A high-quality consultant who is confident in the value they will continue to deliver does not look at the ground, sweat, or avoid eye contact when asking for the order. They professionally and confidently ask for the order and will accept the response.

Handling Objections with Abundance

If you have received a "no" when asking for the order, you are faced with identifying and handling an objection. In some cases, "no" may mean "no," and that ends the journey. In most cases though, an objection is a signal that the customer wants to order; they just have some outstanding concerns. This is where objection-handling skills are essential.

Receiving an objection from a customer is like reaching the edge of a cliff. You can choose to step off the edge and fall out of the deal or turn around and jump back into it. When working with sales teams, I find there are typically four to five main objections they hear when looking to close a deal.

These can vary, but usually I hear:

1. Price,
2. Product/solution quality,
3. Speed of supply,
4. Existing supplier relationship, or
5. Past bad experience with your company.

The most significant risk you face when dealing with objections is being dragged down the maturity index to the position of a vendor. This will be the sole objective of many procurement personas; it is their job to get the best price possible. And how do they do this? They do this by commoditizing potential suppliers, comparing apples with apples, and driving the best price. Often it leads suppliers to offer inferior and more mediocre products and services. These end up creating more cost within their customer's operations through defects, labor costs, and potential safety risks. I do not believe this approach provides the best outcome for you or your customer's business.

Your purpose is to help customers gain the best outcome for their organization, not just helping the procurement manager reach their target.

I have developed a three-step process as shown in Figure 10.9 for handling objections with abundance in a consultative way that maintains the value in the solution for the customer and the salesperson.

Salespeople typically dread price objections. A price objection can pull the relationship perception and your sales approach right back down to the vendor position. To avoid this situation, the first step toward handling a price objection with abundance is to always park it. This is simply achieved by saying with empathy:

> "I can see that price is important to you. Do you mind if we come back to price in a moment? Are there any other concerns or issues you have with moving forward with this project apart from price?"

By making a statement like this, you are acknowledging their concerns about the price in an empathic way. You can then probe to understand if

1. Park Price

2. Root Cause

Why?
Why?
Why?
Why?
Why?

3. Commercial Storytelling

Figure 10.9 Handling Objections with Abundance.

there is anything else that has not been raised that could block the buying process moving forward.

If there are other objections aside from price, it is important to uncover and handle these first, before price. If you don't, you could risk another price objection coming up, which would diminish your closing position. By asking if there are any other concerns about moving forward apart from price, you are moving the deal toward closing. The price objection will be the final step to gaining agreement.

With any issue or concern, it is essential to get to its root causes before trying to solve it. Asking "why" or "what" a few times, for any objection, will bring you to the deeper root cause of the situation.

Typically, with a price objection, I find the flow follows like this:

Issue statement: I am concerned about your pricing.
Question: Why is price so important?
Response: Price is a crucial measure I am focused on.
Question: Why is price something you are focused on?
Response: The CEO is focused on getting our business expenses down.
Question: Why is your CEO currently focused on getting your business expenses down?
Response: Our market is becoming more competitive, and we need to return a profit for our shareholders.

With this flow of questioning around the price, you typically find the root cause or bigger picture links back to company's net profit. Now we are talking about more than just product price; we are talking about total cost, ROI, payback. We are talking about the overall gains your solution will provide the customer's organization. By using root cause questioning, you can elevate the conversation again.

The same root cause questioning technique can be used with any customer objection. It provides you and the customer with insight about the bigger picture around the objection. It will enable you to elevate the conversation again and gear up to tell an appealing commercial story to move the buying journey forward.

The process of telling commercial stories for objections is the same as the process used to build motivation in a deal and lead it toward purchase. Because sales teams typically hear the same few complaints over and over, commercial stories can be pre-developed, packaged, and practiced, gearing the sales team to deliver them well. A future-oriented story reveals the bigger picture in a consultative way. The giving of facts, figures, and next steps enables the purchase to move forward.

Example: Handling Objections

The best case that I have seen of a salesperson using these techniques was within the musical instrument retail industry with a salesperson named Jordan Kouper. The instrument retail industry is highly competitive, with intense levels of online competition. Customer personas are typically price-sensitive and technical experts within their field.

If Jordan received a price objection, he would always acknowledge it using empathic listening. He then probes using root cause questioning, "Do you mind me asking why is pricing a concern for you?" Musician personas Jordan was selling to would have seen a lower price online, and the deeper reason was they had limited disposable income.

With this knowledge, Jordan was able to move into a commercial story he regularly used for this common objection. He focused the conversation, showing empathy, to the significant investment the product posed considering their limited disposable income. Jordan would then tell a future-oriented story or one based on the benefit of a previous customer. He would detail the additional value his company offered musicians, how this would help them gain exposure, build their brand, and generate higher income.

Jordan then proposed the next step moving forward, that payment for the instrument could be spread over an extended period. This helped the customer to purchase the instrument with Jordan and gain greater benefits for the future. This was a great objection-handling process Jordan was able

to use regularly. He ultimately helped the customer in the long run through
the access it provided them over and above the purchase of the instrument.

Every organization is different, but I find that every organization will have
its own common objections they deal with regularly.

To move more customers into the "Delivery" phase of their buying journey, remember to park price, brainstorm common objections and their root
causes, and build commercial stories. These critical sales techniques will
help you and your team stay in the buying journey with more customers,
reducing lost deals and improving sales results.

Suggested Actions for "Purchase"

"Purchase" is the part of the buying journey we all want to reach and succeed with. It is the phase of the buying journey where all the excellent work
we have previously done will come into play and help us to win the deal.

These suggested actions will help you at the "Purchase" phase:

1. Collaborate cross-functionally and review your "Purchase" to "Delivery"
   process to identify barriers. Action improving these to simplify the
   buying journey for your customers.
2. Brainstorm as a team to define your organization's unique points of
   difference and value.
3. Brainstorm as a team some commercial stories built around your unique
   capabilities and past stories of success.
4. Develop some nashis – create the valuable, unique points of difference
   that can be quoted that will differentiate your organization.
5. Practice asking for the order using closed probes to elicit a "yes" or "no"
   response.
6. Brainstorm the common objections the organization receives. Develop
   some commercial stories to overcome these and practice the objection-
   handling process.
7. Develop a coaching and review approach to check improvement
   progress.

Taking these steps will help you and your team improve at this critical stage
of the customer's buying journey.

Chapter 11

Delivery

"Delivery" is the phase of the customer's journey where operational excellence is critical. Customers have made a commitment to purchase from your organization. They are now expecting everything to be delivered as promised. Quality of delivery is paramount when dealing with a new or existing customer. We all experience amazing deliveries with step-by-step product build and delivery communication through text messages, email, or online.

Domino's Pizza is a leader in this space. A customer can purchase a low-cost pizza and monitor their pizza's journey from creation through to delivery, tracking the delivery driver's progress. This is effective communication and customer experience within a commoditized, competitive market. Domino's created a point of difference and continue to improve in the delivery experience for their customers.

Achieving a fantastic delivery journey for customers is not as simple as handing a purchase order over to a delivery team and telling them to do a good job. Customer experiences, like the one achieved by Domino's, are only achieved by a cross-functional team that collaborates closely, continuously improving in an Agile environment. The employees focus on both their internal and external customers and commit to a culture of continuous improvement toward perfection in customer experience and value.

Collaborating to Achieve Excellence in "Delivery"

"Delivery" of a product or service to a customer typically requires more than one team and organization working together to ensure a smooth experience for the end customer. This requires sales, finance, operations, and supply chains to work effectively to provide an excellent outcome for customers. Cross-functional collaboration between sales, operations, supply chain, etc. sounds like a simple concept. We work for the same company; why wouldn't we get on and collaborate? This is one of the most studied and documented areas of business that I am aware of.

Why don't cross-functional teams collaborate? There are many reasons, some of which are:

1. Competing measures between company divisions,
2. Organization silo structures,
3. Poor leadership behaviors, and
4. Lack of internal customer thinking.

I am going to focus on point 4: lack of internal customer thinking. I believe if an organization can build the desire to achieve point 4, and work on it, they have a chance of getting points 1, 2, and 3 right.

Collaborating with Internal Customers

The internal customer concept is about focusing on the next person or team in your process as if they are your customer rather than someone who needs to get something done for you. The reason for this is that it creates higher quality and flow throughout the delivery process. Teams who work to help and improve for their internal customers deliver excellent results in delivery performance and experience for external customers.

What behaviors would this lead to if sales thought of operational teams as their customers as well as the external customer they are trying to sell to? Some examples may be:

■ Greater focus on the accuracy of data they provide operations,
■ Providing timely data,
■ Greater communication throughout the sales process to keep operations informed, and
■ Greater willingness to enter into a dialogue with operations and help when something goes wrong.

Let's think about this concept in reverse. Let's consider a process where operations need to engage sales during the delivery process, providing the salesperson information and samples. If operations looked at the salesperson in this scenario as their internal customer, some behaviors you may see are:

- Drive and energy to hit required timelines for the samples,
- Quality communication and support of the salesperson with the samples, and
- Greater willingness to enter into a dialogue and help when something changes or goes wrong.

Internal customer thinking, as part of an Agile Sales culture, builds greater cross-functional collaboration and ultimately results in amazing delivery experiences for customers. All of the Agile Sales systems discussed in this book so far help in the development of internal customer thinking and collaboration.

The next level of collaboration that can go a long way to creating amazing customer experiences throughout delivery is customer collaboration, which is often called co-creation.

Customer Collaboration – Co-creation

If we are looking to elevate our sales approach and help customers solve problems and improve toward their strategic direction, collaboration during delivery is vital.

Trials/Free Product Samples

Many sales organizations offer customers trials and free product samples as part of their sales process. I believe this approach is flawed as it does not typically create collaboration. Providing a product trial stifles empowerment and ownership with customers. They have been offered this free product or free trial, and they often hand it back saying thanks for the offer but we don't want to move forward. If they do happen to test the product, their commitment to the success of the trial is usually low. They have no skin in the game; irrespective of whether it works or doesn't work, there is limited impact on them.

Pilots

On the other hand, agreeing with a customer to pilot a concept or improvement is a collaborative approach where both parties work together to achieve an improvement. A pilot implies that, together, we will experiment with this improvement, which may require adjustments and changes. A pilot represents a commitment to work through the process together, experimenting together to achieve a set goal or outcome.

Pilots align well with the Sprint concept, which we have previously discussed. Remember the short rapid experiments where customers, salespeople, and technical experts work together? They progress through rapid cycles of planning, doing the experiment, checking if it works, then acting based on the information gained, and repeating the cycle again.

Many great solutions and innovative products have been created in this manner through organizations working together in a co-creation approach.

Example: insignia, Co-creation

One of the best examples I saw was a co-creation approach followed by one of Australia's major mail organization (customer) and insignia (supplier). The goal was to create a step-change within the mail coding and stamp cancellation systems within mail sortation machines. All parties involved from both companies were highly focused on this goal and motivated to achieve a successful outcome. Throughout the delivery process, both companies worked together. The team ran iterative experiments that were focused on innovation in mail coding.

   The team overcame some significant challenges. These challenges would have traditionally derailed a project like this. The co-creation teamwork approach helped them overcome these challenges rather than getting frustrated and stopping the project. The team used PDCA scientific thinking to explore and test improvements to keep the project moving forward. Many improvements were made throughout the delivery process, which resulted in a system that achieved the project's goals, delighted the customer, and achieved ongoing performance for the customer and supplier.

When you are pushing the boundaries of innovation to achieve goals for customers, collaboration and experimentation are required. Co-creation has developed some of the most amazing products we use in our day-to-day lives, from mobile phones and computers to mountain bikes and cars. They have also helped solve major social issues as highlighted in the following example.

Example: Health Industry, Co-creation

I worked on a co-creation project to eliminate errors and speed up the process of blood taking and processing within a significant health department. Many health organizations that need to process blood samples have similar issues that arise from traditional handwritten labeling of blood vials. This health organization had been tracking errors in blood taking for several years and were concerned about the level of errors in this critical process. Each failure could lead to a delay, which may harm a patient. It could also lead to errors in the treatment given to patients. Nurses and other team members involved in blood taking and sampling were also overburdened with no time to spare.

We knew there was a significant improvement to achieve in this area to improve accuracy and save time for the staff. Several challenges were preventing the improvement from moving forward. Some of the difficulties were internal to the health department; others were technology based. These challenges in the past had disrupted the project and stopped any progression at all from being made.

To overcome this, we adopted a co-creation approach backed with a definite purpose. We formed a young team of people with different skill sets from two suppliers and the health organization. From the start, the group agreed that they were making this improvement to improve health outcomes for their community. They all lived in the local area, as did their families. Making an improvement in this area had a significant flow-on effect. It meant that their family members would have a safer higher-quality outcome at these health centers when they most needed it.

The team focused on the purpose of the project rather than purely making money. All parties invested in the technology required to make the solution a reality. They collaborated to overcome challenges that arose and had fantastic communication through the RVM'S (rapid visual meetings) they formed to manage the project in an Agile Sales way. They delivered a solution within three months. This is amazing, considering the project had been stalled for years previously. No one made enormous amounts of money initially, but the suppliers have made good returns over time as the project rolled out to other areas.

The result was an error-proof blood taking process that also saved over 30% of the time required to take and label the blood. This time saving was significant for nurses and other staff involved in blood taking as they gained back precious time. This time saved helped them personally and also helped them focus more on the critical roles and processes they perform every day.

A few years later, my family directly benefited from this improvement. My father was rushed to a hospital in a critical condition after having a heart attack. This was the start of a significant battle for my father to survive. On one visit with my father, he mentioned the technology the nurses used to take and label his blood and how efficient it was. He did not know of the project I had been involved in. When I told him, he called over one of the nurses he had befriended. She told me firsthand of the pressure the system had taken off their workload and the confidence they had in its accuracy. I didn't know during the project that my family would be benefiting from

> this co-creation initiative so soon. I am so grateful that it was in place for my father. I am glad to say that he is alive and well now. He is made of tough stuff, kept on fighting, and made it through. I am sure that the speed and accuracy of blood sampling benefited him greatly.

This project has delivered amazing value and returns to all involved. Perhaps the most significant gains are the social benefits that each and every community with the solution is now experiencing. Sometimes in sales, we look at an opportunity and walk away from it because of its difficulty or perception of lack of value or short-term return. I am glad the team involved in this example did not walk away but instead collaborated and co-created together to achieve amazing results.

Surprise and Delight – The $3 Umbrella

The "Delivery" phase of the customer's journey is a great time to think about surprise and delight opportunities as they are perceived as a highly altruistic offering. In the customer's mind, they have had a great experience with you and your organization already. They have paid their money, and now they are expecting to get exactly what they paid for. When you deliver precisely what they paid for, and add in something over and above, you provide your customer with incredible, unexpected delight.

You may have heard about the $3 umbrella concept. High-quality handbag manufacturers would insert a free umbrella within their handbags during the delivery process. The customer would discover the matching umbrella with a sweet note of thanks accompanying it. These handbags are often worth over $500.00. The umbrella that provides a fantastic experience only costs $3, but the experience it provides the customer is priceless.

For organizations looking to build long-lasting devoted customers, experimentation, and improvement around the $3 umbrella concept can promote you to this level quickly. Many friends have told me about the experience they had purchasing a familiar brand of high-end motorbike. They expected to be handed the keys once they had paid their money but were surprised and delighted to receive free additional inclusions such as riding gloves, branded key rings, and cleaning kits. This made the delivery experience incredible! Surprise and delight approaches don't cost the earth, if anything at all. An organization must place themselves in their customer's shoes. They need to tailor a surprise that will amaze their customers and thus support the journey toward devotion.

Suggested Actions for "Delivery"

"Delivery" is a stage in the customer's buying journey where they can experience amazing delight. It also has the potential to be a source of disappointment for customers if the business is not operating excellently.

Some steps you may consider taking are:

1. Consider your organization's level of maturity with internal customer thinking. What steps could you and your team take to improve internal customer thinking?
2. Have you ever co-created an innovative product or solution with a customer? Is there an existing or target customer that a pilot co-creation approach may deliver value to? What cross-functional team members would you involve from your organization?
3. Consider a surprise and delight technique you could implement. Place yourself in the persona of focus shoes and consider their experience.

Improving in this area of "Delivery" will help you move toward the "Devotion" phase more quickly. "Devotion" in a customer's buying journey is the stage that we all want to reach. It is the state where the customer will not consider other options; they are devoted to you and your company.

Chapter 12

Devotion

"Devotion" is an awesome place to be, where your customers are devoted to your brand. This is a place of customer satisfaction and delight so supreme that they will continue to move through their buying journeys with you and your organization evermore.

How can you build devotion with a customer, so that they never consider another provider? I can offer the following two scenarios and will concentrate on these during this chapter.

1. Utilize a cyclical value-adding customer engagement approach that keeps providing a tailored experience that helps customers overcome challenges and achieve their goals.
2. Develop a tailored surprise and delight approach ongoing (even when customers are not in a buying journey).

Cyclical Value-Adding Customer Engagement Approach

Traditionally, we have thought of a sales process as being a linear approach that has several steps and a definitive start and finish. Very few buying journeys of customers are like this. Instead, they resemble more of a loop or cycle, much like a biological cycle that keeps repeating itself. When an organization thinks in cyclical rather than linear systems, they open up the opportunity to innovate ongoing for customers, providing a value-added, delightful buying journey.

Let's consider a customer looking to obtain a loan from a financial institution. They are going to enter a buying journey, which will result in them choosing a loan provider. We could look at this sale as a once-off event. Or we could consider the more profound reason a customer requires a loan and the financial journey they embark upon throughout their life. This will most certainly involve many changes and buying journeys.

Firstly, using root cause thinking, let's consider the deeper reason a person obtains a loan:

Why does a customer purchase a loan?
They need money.

Why do they need money?
They wish to make a purchase.

Why do they want to make a purchase?
They want to progress in life.

Why do they want to progress in life?
They want to provide for their family.

Why do they want to provide for their family?
They care for, love, and want the best for their family.

I would imagine that this is quite a common story. Considering this purpose, a whole new perspective on the true meaning of providing finance is revealed. When you think about this deeper reasoning, it is easy to reflect on the many cycles a financial institution could use to improve its customers' experience during their life. A financial institution that focuses its energy on continuously helping its customers provide the best for their family will enter many buying cycles (Figure 12.1).

How should a financial organization develop a cyclical customer engagement approach that will generate a lifelong partnership with customers? There is undoubtedly the need for it considering a customer's financial journey throughout their life.

Signet's Process Optimization Program (Figure 10.7) provides details of an industrial/supply chain cyclical partnership approach for supporting and helping customers throughout their journey. A cyclical ongoing value-adding customer engagement approach can be developed for virtually any industry and customer persona. One must understand their customers first, live in their shoes, then look at aligning their own present and future organizational capability to this.

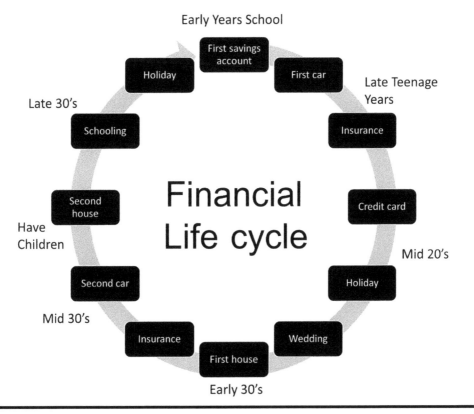

Figure 12.1 Financial Life Cycle.

Ongoing Surprise and Delight

Providing customers continuous surprise and delight will go a long way to building devotion. A famous contributor to this theory is Noriaki Kano, a professor at the Tokyo University of Science. In the late 1970s and early 1980s, Kano (Noriaki Kano, 1984) and his colleagues laid the foundation for a new approach to modeling customer satisfaction, which became known as the Kano model (Figure 12.2).

Kano used a two-quadrant chart to describe the findings of his model. A customer's satisfaction level was plotted against an organization's quality of execution at delivering value. What he found was the experiences that delight a customer need to be repeatable to sustain delight. If a customer receives a delightful experience one day and then does not the next time they engage with a supplier, their perception will quickly drop to the basic level.

Consider you take your car in for a well-priced service. You expect that they will service your vehicle and get it back to you on time. When you

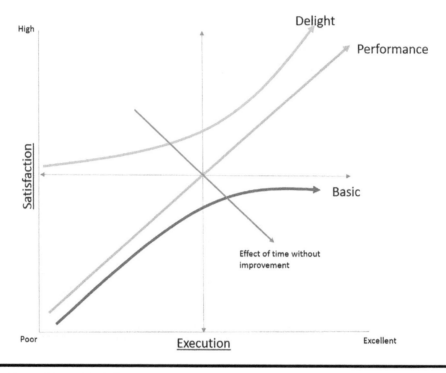

Figure 12.2   Kano Model.

pick up your vehicle, you see that they have thoroughly cleaned it! The car is shining, the tires are blackened, and the interior vacuumed and cleaned. How do you feel? … DELIGHTED!

What if you then took the vehicle back to that service provider six months later? You have held off cleaning your car, knowing the service provider cleaned it as part of the last service and expecting them to repeat this. You have told all your friends and colleagues at work about this service provider, proud of having found such a fantastic business. When you turn up later that day to pick up your car, you find it still dirty and not cleaned. How do you feel now? … DISAPPOINTED!

A service is delightful only if it can be repeated.

The other phenomenon that Kano found was that a delightful experience over time will reduce in perception. It could fall to a level of performance or even a basic requirement.

Consider that you have been taking your car to the same service provider for five years and each time you get the car back clean. Does the clean car provide you the same level of delight five years down the track as it did the first few times? … No!

Delivering ongoing delight requires sustaining the delightful factors you have previously provided and continuously improving to offer new delightful experiences over time. Consider that for two years, you have been taking your car to the same service provider and each time it comes back clean. On the fourth occasion, you drop the car off for a service expecting to get it back spotless and ready to drive away. When you turn up that afternoon, you find the car clean and ready to drive away. But you also discover a handwritten card on the driver's seat thanking you for being a customer for two years with a $10 scratch-and-win ticket attached. How do you feel now? … DELIGHTED!

This repeatable innovative approach to delight is the secret to helping customers build devotion to your brand. Delivering on it is not easy. It requires us to be highly systematic and diligent to ensure we keep repeating with accuracy the delightful experience. It also requires us to continue to innovate to deliver new repeatable delightful experiences into the future. Again, the Agile Sales techniques we have covered within this book will help you achieve this as an organization.

Suggested Actions for "Devotion"

"Devotion" is the stage in the buying journey that we want our customers to reach with our brand. This is not a simple process.

Considering the following actions could help you to build your approach to achieving devotion with your customers:

1. Conduct a Root Cause Analysis of why your customers purchase the products and services you sell.
2. As a team, map the life cycle of the customer's buying journey throughout their life for these products and services.
3. Consider a cyclical sales framework/process that you could develop to help align with this journey ongoing.
4. Place yourself in your customer's shoes and think about the things that would delight them. Run these ideas through a PICK chart, and choose one to implement systematically so that it is repeatable.
5. Track development of the process that brings delight to customers within your team's rapid visual meeting (RVM). Set a timeframe to organize the next delighting improvement.

Improving in this area of "Devotion" will build long-lasting customer relationships, which will bring significantly more value over time than once-off purchases. These devoted customers can also be leveraged to help you discover more potential customers to move through a buying journey to "Devotion." We will explore "Leveraging" now.

Chapter 13

Leveraging

It has been 20 years since my university days! I still remember like it was yesterday, a marketing lecturer standing up in front of the lecture theatre with a CD. (He would have displayed the Spotify app in today's age.) He said that if we remember one thing from his course and one thing alone, remember to "leverage." He gave the example of a musician who writes a song, records it once, and then leverages it many times by putting the songs on a CD which is sold time and time again. This is how you make money, he said. To me, "Leveraging" your successes, and unique processes you have created, is a crucial element of continuous improvement (CI).

There are three elements of "Leveraging" that I would like to offer in enabling you and your company to leverage into the future:

1. Process,
2. Customer, and
3. People.

Leveraging Your Sales Process

Customers are looking for organizations that will help them, over the long term, to improve their journey. The key is to have an approach designed and integrated as part of your culture that allows you to deliver on this. Let's think about leveraging your sales process, in comparison to a music CD.

1. Developing the standard value-added sales approach, that is aligned to the customer buying journey, is the same as writing the song.
2. Putting effort into training, coaching, measuring, and forming the process habits within your team is like recording the CD.
3. Repeating it many times over, with everything you do, equates to the marketing and selling of the artist's CD time and time again.

The beauty with process and standards is that you can keep improving them continuously into the future, making them better and more successful. This does not always apply to record artists and their songs.

Leveraging Customers

"Leveraging" customers involves building upon the successes you have with a customer who has received considerable value and delight and is willing to talk about it. There is no more powerful lead generator than word of mouth; a person from one company speaks to a person in a similar role within another company. You have the power to enable this process by providing these delighted, advocating customers the forum to speak.

You could develop case studies and references from these customers. You could help them to promote themselves and the achievements both within their own organization and externally through social media, industry groups, etc. You could facilitate industry and educational events where other people can come along, network, and learn from your customers directly. You could promote events where your delighted customers speak about the great experience and fantastic value they have delivered in partnership with you and your organization. There is no more powerful lead generation technique.

Leveraging People

"Leveraging" people is about keeping in touch with the people within the companies where you have had success. Programs such as LinkedIn and CRM (customer relationship management) packages are great tools that enable this. If your company runs a cyclical value-adding sales and account management process, you will be building highly revered "partnership" relationships. These partners will continue to grow and expand their careers into the future, often within similar industries and companies. As they grow in their careers within an organization, it provides an opportunity to leverage the success you have previously had with these people, strengthening your relationship as their trusted partner. Keeping track of and in contact with these people is the key to sustaining these trusted partnership relationships and is surprisingly easy to implement using CRM packages and programs like LinkedIn.

Example: Leveraging People

A fantastic approach to leveraging people was developed by Boyd Rose, a high-performance salesman with whom I worked. Boyd exudes humility and always focuses on achieving value-adding outcomes and improvements for customers. Boyd developed a newsletter-style approach to help him keep in touch with his cohort of customers and prospects. He would send this newsletter via email as an electronic direct mail (EDM).

The difference with the approach Boyd took was the personal, open structure to the communication. Boyd always began the email with an update on himself and his family. He included photos and then went on to provide some value-added information concerning industry data, knowledge, CI elements, etc. He kept the EDM short and straightforward, containing no more than three points in each communication. All three points were to be of great value to the customer and not just a sales pitch.

Boyd was passionate about not spamming his customers, as this would devalue the EDM for them. This regular correspondence led to a high open and response rate for Boyd's process. It helped Boyd maintain contact and relationships with a large cohort of customers and potential customers through this personal value-added communication. While I have seen similar systems fail, Boyd's approach differed in that he was being humble and open, providing value-added information, and minimizing the "sales" talk.

Suggested Actions for Leveraging

The greatest "Discovery" technique is your existing devoted customers. Consider the following actions to start leveraging your success:

1. Develop your own cyclical sales process that aligns with your customer's lifetime buying journey.

2. Who are the devoted customers you already have? Can you develop case studies for them and run events they will speak at for you? Would they allow site tours for other potential customers?
3. Consider how you keep in touch with your devoted customers into the future. How strong are you at using LinkedIn and systematically touching base with past contacts?

Improving in this area of leveraging will help you sustain "Devotion" while at the same time amplifying your "Discovery" efforts for new personas to take through a buying journey. This is one of the most straightforward, practical approaches to delivering ongoing value and delight for your customers and yourself.

Conclusion

Delivering customer journeys of value and delight requires a continuously improving, customer-centric Agile Sales organization. Without this, it will be difficult to continuously innovate to deliver new delightful experiences for customers into the future. Change in our world today is not slowing down. It seems as though the pace of change will continue to increase, and organizations will need to evolve to keep up.

Customers, through their buying decisions determine the success or failure of an organization. The decisions being made by customers are based on the experience they receive from our front-line teams and systems. The knowledge and skills both practically and emotionally of our front-line teams is so crucial, as it is through these people that success or failure will be achieved. Customer experience is one of the last sustainable points of difference.

If you and your team can develop unique approaches to deliver higher value and delight for customers than your competition and continuously improve to sustain this position, you will achieve great things. My recommendation is that the best way to explore how to achieve this is to involve your customers and front-line teams who are engaging customers every day.

The seven Agile Sales concepts will develop the systems within your organization to enable continuous focus on customers and front-line teams. These systems will provide your whole organization a way of capturing new ideas and executing these daily while sustaining focus on achieving your strategic goals. The seven Agile Sales concepts will provide mechanisms to know, at any given time, where you are succeeding and where you face challenges. These systems will give you and your team these insights well ahead of traditional lag-measure-oriented review systems focused purely on sales/budget results.

As more organizations embrace an Agile Sales approach, new innovative ideas and concepts will arise. This book has been written at a moment in time based on the current knowledge available. We have covered extensively within this book the continuously improving nature of Agile Sales. New techniques, skills, and capabilities will continue to evolve out of this approach as teams continually work to improve the value and delight they provide customers.

I invite your interaction via my website blog at iqi.com.au. Please feel free to link and engage through the site's blog to share your experience and ideas about Agile Sales to help others grow and develop toward excellence. Let's all work together to get salespeople back in the game, delivering higher value and delight to customers and success for themselves, their families, and organizations!

Bibliography

Brown, B. (2014). *The Power of Vulnerability*. Houston: TEDx.

Carnegie, D. (2006). *How to Win Friends and Influence People*. London: Vermilion.

Caskey, B. and Neale, B. (2019). The Advanced Selling Podcast. Indiana.

Covey, S. R. (1989). *The 7 Habits of Highly Effective People*. London: Simon & Shuster UK Ltd.

Deming, W. E. (1982). *Out of the Crisis*. Cambridge: MIT Center for Advanced Educational Services.

Dennis, P. (2006). *Getting the Right Things Done*. Cambridge: Lean Enterprises Inst Inc.

Dobelli, R. (2014). *The Art of Thinking Clearly*. London: Sceptre.

Hines, P. and Butterworth, C. (2019). *The Essence of Excellence*. Caerphilly: SA Partners.

King, M. L. (1963). "I Have a Dream" Speech. Washington, DC.

Luketic, R. (2001). Legally Blond Film.

Nonaka, H. T. and Takeuchi, H. (1986). The New Product Development Game. *Harvard Business Review*. 64(1):137–46.

Noriaki Kano, S. N. (1984). Attractive Quality and Must-be Quality. *Journal of the Japanese Society for Quality Control*. 14(2):39–48.

Pareto, V. (1896). *Cous d'Economie Politique*. Lauranne: l'Universite de Lausanne.

Rifkin, J. (2010). *The Empathic Civilisation*. Cambridge: Polity Press.

Ritzer, G. (2008). *The McDonaldization of Society 5*. Los Angeles: Pine Forge Press.

Schwaber, K. and Sutherland, J. (2016). SCRUM Guide. Self Published.

Shmook, N. (2017). *Three Words Powering Richmond*. https://www.richmondfc.com.au/news/304764/three-words-powering-richmond.

Index

For Product Safety Concerns and Information please contact our EU
representative GPSR@taylorandfrancis.com
Taylor & Francis Verlag GmbH, Kaufingerstraße 24, 80331 München, Germany

www.ingramcontent.com/pod-product-compliance
Ingram Content Group UK Ltd.
Pitfield, Milton Keynes, MK11 3LW, UK
UKHW050931180425
457613UK00015B/360